Marianne Jewell Memorial Library
Baker College of Muskegon
Muskegon, Michigan 49442

BAKER COLLEGE LIBRARY

3 3504 00471 6157

KF 3775 .A7 E57 2006

The environment

DATE DUE

D1451659

The Environment

Other books in the Issues on Trial series:

The Environment

Andrea C. Nakaya, Book Editor

GREENHAVEN PRESS

An imprint of Thomson Gale, a part of The Thomson Corporation

THOMSON
—————✳—————™
GALE

Detroit • New York • San Francisco • San Diego • New Haven, Conn.
Waterville, Maine • London • Munich

Marianne Jewell Memorial Library
Baker College of Muskegon
Muskegon, Michigan 49442

The Environment

Publisher	Series Editor	Managing Editor
Bonnie Szumski	Scott Barbour	Helen Cothran

©2006 Thomson Gale, a part of The Thomson Corporation.

Thomson and Star Logo are trademarks and Gale and Greenhaven Press are registered trademarks used herein under license.

For more information, contact:
Greenhaven Press
27500 Drake Rd.
Farmington Hills, MI 48331-3535
Or you can visit our Internet site at http://www.gale.com

Greenhaven Press anthologies primarily consist of previously published material taken from a variety of sources, including periodicals, books, scholarly journals, newspapers, government documents, and position papers from private and public organizations. These original sources are often edited for length and to ensure their accessibility for a young adult audience. The anthology editors also change the original titles of these works in order to clearly present the main thesis of each viewpoint and to explicitly indicate the opinion presented in the viewpoint. These alterations were made in consideration of both the reading and comprehension levels of a young adult audience. Every effort has been made to ensure that Greenhaven Press accurately reflects the original intent of the authors included in this anthology.

ALL RIGHTS RESERVED
No part of this work covered by the copyright hereon may be reproduced or used in any form or by any means—graphic, electronic, or mechanical, including photocopying, recording, taping, Web distribution, or information storage retrieval systems—without the written permission of the publisher.

For permission to use material from this product, submit your request via the Web at http://www.gale-edit.com/permissions, or you may download our Permissions Request form and submit your request by fax or mail to:

Permissions Department
Thomson Gale
27500 Drake Rd.
Farmington Hills, MI 48331-3535
Permissions Hotline:
248-699-8006 or 800-877-4253, ext. 8006
Fax: 248-699-8074 or 800-762-4048

Since this page cannot legibly accommodate all copyright notices, the acknowledgements constitute an extension of the copyright notice.

Cover photograph reproduced by permission of © Louis Schwartzberg/CORBIS.

While every effort has been made to ensure the reliability of the information presented in this publication, Thomson Gale does not guarantee the accuracy of the data contained herein. Thomson Gale accepts no payment for listing; and inclusion in the publication of any organization, agency, institution, publication, service, or individual does not imply endorsement by the editors or publisher. Errors brought to the attention of the publisher and verified to the satisfaction of the publisher will be corrected in future editions.

LIBRARY OF CONGRESS CATALOGING-IN-PUBLICATION DATA

The environment / Andrea C. Nakaya, book editor.
    p. cm. -- (Issues on Trial)
    Includes bibliographical references and index.
    ISBN 0-7377-2797-7 (lib. : alk. paper)
    1. Environmental law--United States--Cases. I. Nakaya, Andrea C., 1976– II. Series.
    KF3775.A7E57 2006
    344.7304'6--dc22
                           2005052713

Contents

Chapter 1: Upholding Citizens' Right to Protect the Environment

   Paul Raymond Hays

   In *Scenic Hudson Preservation Conference v. Federal
   Power Commission* (1965) the Second Circuit Court of
   Appeals decided that citizens may sue to protect nature and that the government must make efforts to preserve natural resources when developing public land.

   Glenn Fowler

   A newspaper editorialist writing in 1969 argues that
   environmental protection must be balanced with competing societal needs, such as an increasing demand
   for electric power.

   Natural Resources Defense Council

   An environmental organization asserts that *Scenic Hudson* established the legitimacy of environmental issues
   in the courts.

   Philip Weinberg

   A law professor opines that while this 1965 case established the right of conservationists to file environmental lawsuits, that right has been greatly eroded by the
   courts since then.

Chapter 2: Balancing Wildlife Management Against Economic Interests

Chapter 3: Balancing Private Property Rights Against Environmental Conservation

Foreword

The U.S. courts have long served as a battleground for the most highly charged and contentious issues of the time. Divisive matters are often brought into the legal system by activists who feel strongly for their cause and demand an official resolution. Indeed, subjects that give rise to intense emotions or involve closely held religious or moral beliefs lay at the heart of the most polemical court rulings in history. One such case was *Brown v. Board of Education* (1954), which ended racial segregation in schools. Prior to *Brown*, the courts had held that blacks could be forced to use separate facilities as long as these facilities were equal to that of whites.

For years many groups had opposed segregation based on religious, moral, and legal grounds. Educators produced heartfelt testimony that segregated schooling greatly disadvantaged black children. They noted that in comparison to whites, blacks received a substandard education in deplorable conditions. Religious leaders such as Martin Luther King Jr. preached that the harsh treatment of blacks was immoral and unjust. Many involved in civil rights law, such as Thurgood Marshall, called for equal protection of all people under the law, as their study of the Constitution had indicated that segregation was illegal and un-American. Whatever their motivation for ending the practice, and despite the threats they received from segregationists, these ardent activists remained unwavering in their cause.

Those fighting against the integration of schools were mainly white southerners who did not believe that whites and blacks should intermingle. Blacks were subordinate to whites, they maintained, and society had to resist any attempt to break down strict color lines. Some white southerners charged that segregated schooling was *not* hindering blacks' education. For example, Virginia attorney general J. Lindsay Almond asserted, "With the help and the sympathy and the love and respect of the white people of the South, the colored man has risen under that educational process to a place of eminence and respect throughout the nation. It has served him well." So when the Supreme Court ruled against the segregationists in *Brown*, the South responded with vociferous cries of protest. Even government leaders criticized the decision. The governor of Arkansas, Orval Faubus, stated that he would not "be a party to any attempt to force acceptance of change to which the people are so overwhelmingly opposed." Indeed, resistance to integration was so great that when black students arrived at the formerly all-white Central High School in Arkansas, federal troops had to be dispatched to quell a threatening mob of protesters.

Nevertheless, the *Brown* decision was enforced and the South integrated its schools. In this instance, the Court, while not settling the issue to everyone's satisfaction, functioned as an instrument of progress by forcing a major social change. Historian David Halberstam observes that the *Brown* ruling "deprived segregationist practices of their moral legitimacy. . . . It was therefore perhaps the single most important moment of the decade, the moment that separated the old order from the new and helped create the tumultuous era just arriving." Considered one of the most important victories for civil rights, *Brown* paved the way for challenges to racial segregation in many areas, including on public buses and in restaurants.

In examining *Brown*, it becomes apparent that the courts play an influential role—and face an arduous challenge—in shaping the debate over emotionally charged social issues. Judges must balance competing interests, keeping in mind the high stakes and intense emotions on both sides. As exemplified by *Brown*, judicial decisions often upset the status quo and initiate significant changes in society. Greenhaven Press's Issues on Trial series captures the controversy surrounding influential court rulings and explores the social ramifications of such decisions from varying perspectives. Each anthology highlights one social issue—such as the death penalty, students' rights, or wartime civil liberties. Each volume then focuses on key historical and contemporary court cases that helped mold the issue as we know it today. The books include a compendium of primary sources—court rulings, dissents, and immediate reactions to the rulings—as well as secondary sources from experts in the field, people involved in the cases, legal analysts, and other commentators opining on the implications and legacy of the chosen cases. An annotated table of contents, an in-depth introduction, and prefaces that overview each case all provide context as readers delve into the topic at hand. To help students fully probe the subject, each volume contains book and periodical bibliographies, a comprehensive index, and a list of organizations to contact. With these features, the Issues on Trial series offers a well-rounded perspective on the courts' role in framing society's thorniest, most impassioned debates.

Introduction

In 1976 the U.S. Supreme Court heard a case involving a species of three-inch-long fish called the snail darter. According to scientists, the last place on earth where this species lived in significant numbers was the Little Tennessee River in Tennessee. The Tennessee Valley Authority (TVA), however, was in the process of constructing the Tellico Dam on that river. The TVA made a convincing case for the construction of the dam, arguing that it would significantly benefit the area through the creation of hydroelectric power, shoreline development, and flood control. However, conservationists, led by Hiram Hill, also made a persuasive argument. If the dam were completed, the snail darter would be destroyed forever. In *Tennessee Valley Authority v. Hill et al.* the conflict was resolved by the Supreme Court, which decided that since the snail darter was an endangered species it must be protected; therefore, the dam could not be completed. As this case illustrates, American society frequently faces difficult choices between environmental protection and other interests, such as economic development and community welfare. In many cases there are compelling arguments made on both sides, with neither party willing to compromise. In such cases, the courts play an important role by serving as an arbiter between conflicting interest groups. Examining court cases, therefore, can offer insight into the issues involved in some of America's most important environmental conflicts.

In American society, views on the environment range between two extremes. Some environmentalists believe that natural resources such as wilderness areas, clean water, and biological diversity are priceless and should receive absolute protection. For example, author Chester James Antieau maintains that the environment is so important that it is worthy of constitutional protection. "Every person in the United States has an inalienable right to a clean and healthful environment," he asserts. Conservationists such as Antieau argue that if businesses and private landowners are not forced to practice conservation, they will eventually destroy the environment. As environmental experts Michael E. Kraft and Norman J. Vig explain, "Self-interested individuals and a free economic marketplace guided mainly by a concern for short-term profits tend to create . . . pollution. . . . The scope and urgency of environmental problems typically exceed the capacity of private markets and individual efforts to deal with them effectively."

Critics contend that economic growth, employment, and technological development are also important—sometimes more important than conservation. These critics argue that in some cases, the benefits of environmental regulations are not worth the threat they pose to the economic well-being of society. Author Jon Roush explains some of the negative effects of these regulations. "[Conservation policies] restrict access to resources and limit their use," he says. "They demand that people not use available technologies and materials. They claim benefits that are obscure and hard to prove." Many of these conservation critics also believe that environmental regulations threaten the freedom of individuals to do as they wish in their own homes and on their own property. Property rights expert John D. Echeverria explains this logic: "Protection of individual property rights is . . . an important American value, enshrined in the U.S. Constitution," he says. "For many, the right to use one's property . . . is an essential ingredient of the liberty that each American enjoys."

Obviously, society must find a compromise between complete environmental preservation and complete freedom for industry. As Jon Roush points out in his introduction to *Let the People Judge,* even the most stringent defenders of conservation or business realize that such a compromise is necessary. "No one—not even the most dedicated environmentalists—wants to go without food, shelter, and a livelihood," explains Roush, and "no one—not even the most dedicated industrialist or miner—wants to go without clean air and water and green places."

However, there is rarely agreement on where that compromise lies. For this reason, the courts play an important role in environmental disputes. They serve as an arbiter between parties who hold conflicting views of how the environment should be treated. For example, in *TVA v. Hill* the Supreme Court became responsible for assessing the potential benefits of the Tellico Dam and deciding whether these benefits were more important than the existence of the snail darter.

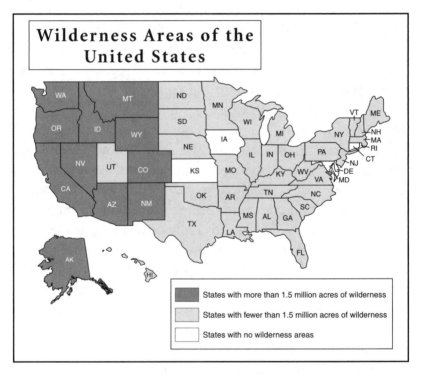

Wilderness Areas of the United States

Through its court decisions, American society is able to find a middle ground between conflicting views about how society should treat the environment. According to author and professor Lettie McSpadden, many of America's environmental protections are the result of court decisions. She says,

Judicial decisions ... [have been important] over the past

two and a half decades in shaping environmental policies from water pollution control to endangered species. Were it not for court injunctions, even fewer ancient trees would be surviving in the United States. Were it not for enforcement actions brought by citizen activists, our waters would be more choked by industrial wastes than they are.

At the same time, though, the courts have continually weighed this environmental protection against the preservation of individual freedom and a healthy economy, sometimes ruling that environmental regulations are undesirable because they harm that freedom or unfairly restrict the economy.

Regardless of which side is favored by the courts' decisions, examining the court cases reveals the essence of many conflicts that exist about America's environment. For example, *TVA v. Hill* illustrates the continuing conflict between conservationists and those wishing to use environmental resources for financial gain. This anthology examines four important court cases involving America's environment: *Scenic Hudson Preservation Conference v. Federal Power Commission* (1965), *Seattle Audubon Society v. John L. Evans and Washington Contract Loggers Association* (1991), *Lucas v. South Carolina Coastal Council* (1992), and *Babbitt v. Sweet Home Chapter of Communities for a Great Oregon* (1995). By offering analyses of the significance and the impact of these cases, the authors highlight the issues America faces in its ongoing relationship with the environment.

Upholding Citizens' Right to Protect the Environment

Case Overview

Scenic Hudson Preservation Conference v. Federal Power Commission (1965)

Many conservationists in the United States use lawsuits as a tool for protecting the environment. For example, when businesses unlawfully pollute the air or water, or when federal agencies fail to adequately enforce pollution laws, environmentalists often sue them in court. Before the late 1960s, however, such lawsuits were rare. In fact, there were few laws or agencies existing to protect America's environment. A 1965 court case, *Scenic Hudson Preservation Conference v. Federal Power Commission,* is often cited as a pivotal case in the history of environmental law. For the first time, a federal court recognized the right of citizens to go to court to protect nature. This case also marked the first federal ruling holding that the government must make efforts to preserve natural resources when developing public land.

In 1965 the Consolidated Edison Company (Con Ed) obtained a license from the Federal Power Commission to construct an electric generating system on Storm King Mountain and the Hudson River in New York State. Conservationists, however, opposed the plan on the grounds that it would threaten the natural resources and beauty of this historic area and formed the Scenic Hudson Preservation Conference to fight Con Ed's plan. After the commission denied the conference's application for a reconsideration of the license, the case went to the Second Circuit Court of Appeals.

The *Scenic Hudson* decision established three precedents. One involved the concept of "standing to sue," which holds that only persons or groups with a particular injury can present their arguments in court. Prior to that case, standing often presented a barrier to citizens and groups attempting to initiate environmental lawsuits because the courts held that to demonstrate standing to sue, a party must possess a concrete, economic interest in a matter. The desire to preserve natural resources was not considered a concrete interest. In 1965, however, the Second Circuit Court changed the criteria for standing when it ruled that the Preservation Conference did have standing to sue due to its desire to protect the natural beauty of the Hudson River.

The second precedent established by *Scenic Hudson* was the use of environmental impact statements. The court ruled that if it did decide to issue a development license to Con Ed, the Federal Power Commission must be prepared to defend its decision with a study evaluating the project's potential effects on the environment.

Finally, the third precedent was set when the Second Circuit Court held that when developing public land such as Storm King Mountain and the Hudson River, the government must balance economic importance with environmental preservation. The court decided that in addition to the economic value of the proposed plant, the Federal Power Commission must also consider its impact on the natural beauty and resources of Storm King Mountain and the Hudson River.

After being sent back to the commission for further consideration, the case went back to court numerous times before Con Ed finally gave up its plan to build the plant in December 1980. However, the 1965 decision was an important judgment that formed a cornerstone of environmental protection in the United States. Author Michael Kitzmiller calls it "one of the great modern conservation victories." According to lawyer Stephen P. Duggan, "the whole body of later environmental legislation began with that single decision, which had demonstrated the capacity of judges to weigh in the scales of justice such questions as ecological balance, preservation of species, and potential pollution." Following the precedent set by *Scenic Hudson,* later court decisions further expanded opportunities for environmental groups to bring issues to the courts. As a result, environmental organizations filed hundreds of citizen suits against the federal and state governments and private industry during the 1970s, achieving some of their most significant judicial victories and making a lasting impact on America's environment.

More recently the courts have been less supportive of lawsuits by conservationists. However, their support in the 1970s was crucial to the development of America's major environmental laws and agencies. *Scenic Hudson* and subsequent cases enabled environmentalists to use litigation to bring pressure on Congress and administrative agencies for more effective environmental policies. The statutes and legal institutions that were created during that decade serve as the fundamental building blocks for environmental policy in the United States today.

"Those who ... have exhibited a special interest in [conservation of the Hudson River have] ... a legal right to protect their special interests."

The Court's Decision: Individuals Can Sue to Protect the Environment

Paul Raymond Hays

On December 29, 1965, the United States Court of Appeals for the Second Circuit ruled in favor of conservationists in Scenic Hudson Preservation Conference v. Federal Power Commission. *The court declared that in deciding whether to allow a hydroelectric plant on the Hudson River in New York, the Federal Power Commission must consider the environmental impact of the plant. In the following excerpt Paul Raymond Hays draws two broad conclusions. First, he argues that while citizens, such as those composing the Scenic Hudson Preservation Conference, have a right to sue to protect their economic interests, they also have a right to protest actions that threaten noneconomic interests such as natural resources, natural beauty, and historic sites. He dismisses fears that his decision will lead to thousands of future environmental lawsuits, arguing that the expense and difficulty of such proceedings will serve to limit them. Second, he contends that in considering Consolidated Edison's application to build the plant, the Federal Power Commission must evaluate the environmental impact of the project in addition to its economic importance. He concludes that before it can approve the proposed plant, the commission must hear the Preservation*

Paul Raymond Hays, opinion, *Scenic Hudson Preservation Conference v. Federal Power Commission,* 354 F.2d 608, December 29, 1965.

Conference's evidence of possible environmental harm and must consider alternatives that might help preserve the beauty and the natural resources of the Hudson River while providing electricity for New York. Hays served on the United States Court of Appeals for the Second Circuit from 1962 to 1980. He died on February 13, 1980.

In this proceeding the petitioners are the Scenic Hudson Preservation Conference, an unincorporated association consisting of a number of non-profit, conservationist organizations, and the Towns of Cortlandt, Putnam Valley and Yorktown. Petitioners ask us, pursuant to § 313(b) of the Federal Power Act, to set aside three orders of the respondent, the Federal Power Commission:

(a) An order of March 9, 1965, granting a license to . . . the Consolidated Edison Company of New York, Inc., to construct a pumped storage hydroelectric project of the west side of the Hudson River at Storm King Mountain in Cornwall, New York;

(b) An order of May 6, 1965, denying petitioners' application for a rehearing of the March 9 order, and for the reopen ing of the proceeding to permit the introduction of addi tional evidence;

(c) An order of May 6, 1965, denying joint motions filed by the petitioners to expand the scope of supplemental hearings to include consideration of the practicality and cost of underground transmission lines, and of the feasibility of *any* type of fish protection device.

The Proposed Storm King Project

A pumped storage plant generates electric energy for use during peak load periods, using hydroelectric units driven by water from a headwater pool or reservoir. The contemplated Storm King project would be the largest of its kind in the world. Consolidated Edison has estimated its cost, including transmission facilities, at $162,000,000. The project would consist of three major components, a storage reservoir, a powerhouse, and transmission lines. The storage reservoir, located over a thousand feet above the powerhouse, is to be connected to the powerhouse, located on the river front, by a tunnel 40 feet in diameter. The powerhouse, which is both a pumping and generating station, would be 800 feet long and contain eight pump generators.

Transmission lines would run under the Hudson to the east bank and then underground for 1.6 miles to a switching station which Consolidated Edison would build at Nelsonville in the Town of Philipstown. Thereafter, overhead transmission lines would be placed on towers 100 to 150 feet high and these would require a path up to 125 feet wide through Westchester and Putnam Counties for a distance of some 25 miles until they reached Consolidated Edison's main connections with New York City.

During slack periods Consolidated Edison's conventional steam plants in New York City would provide electric power for the pumps at Storm King to force water up the mountain, through the tunnel, and into the upper reservoir. In peak periods water would be released to rush down the mountain and power the generators . . . . When pumping the powerhouse would draw approximately 1,080,000 cubic feet of water per minute from the Hudson, and when generating would discharge up to 1,620,000 cubic feet of water per minute into the river. The installation would have a capacity of 2,000,000 kilowatts, but would be so constructed as to be capable of enlargement to a total of 3,000,000 kilowatts. The water in the upper reservoir may be regarded as the equivalent of stored electric energy; in effect, Consolidated Edison wishes to create a huge storage battery at Cornwall . . . .

The Storm King project has aroused grave concern among conservationist groups, adversely affected municipalities and various state and federal legislative units and administrative agencies.

The Need to Consider All Alternatives

To be licensed by the Commission a prospective project must meet the statutory test of being "best adapted to a comprehensive plan for improving or developing a waterway," [as stated in federal law]. In framing the issue before it, the Federal Power Commission properly noted: "We must compare the Cornwall project with any alternatives that are available. If on this record Con Edison has available an alternative source for meeting its power needs which is better adapted to the development of the Hudson River for all beneficial uses, including scenic beauty, this application should be denied."

If the Commission is properly to discharge its duty in this regard, the record on which it bases its determination must be complete. The petitioners and the public at large have a right to demand this completeness. It is our view, and we find, that the Commission has failed to compile a record which is sufficient to support its decision. The Commission has ignored certain relevant factors and failed to make a thorough study of possible alternatives to the Storm King project. While the courts have no authority to concern themselves with the policies of the Commission, it is their duty to see to it that the Commission's decisions receive that careful consideration which the statute contemplates . . . . We set aside the three orders of the Commission to which the petition is addressed and remand the case for further proceedings in accordance with this opinion.

Importance of Preserving Natural Beauty

The Storm King project is to be located in an area of unique beauty and major historical significance. The highlands and gorge of the Hudson offer one of the finest pieces of river scenery in the world. The great German traveler [Karl] Baedeker called it "finer than the Rhine." Petitioners' contention that the Commission must take these factors into consideration in evaluating the Storm King project is justified by the history of the Federal Power Act.

The Federal Water Power Act of 1920, was the outgrowth of a widely supported effort on the part of conservationists to secure the enactment of a complete scheme of national regulation which would promote the comprehensive development of the nation's water resources . . . .

Section 10(a) of the Federal Power Act, reads: . . .

"All licenses issued under . . . this title shall be on the following conditions: (a) That the project adopted, . . . shall be such as in the judgment of the Commission *will be best adopted to a comprehensive plan for improving or developing a waterway or waterways for the use or benefit of interstate or foreign commerce, for the improvement and utilization of water-power development, and for other beneficial public uses, including recreational purposes;* and if necessary in order to secure such plan the Commission shall have authority to require the modification of any project and of the plans and specifications of the project works before approval." (Emphasis added)

"Recreational purposes" are expressly included among the beneficial public uses to which the statute refers. The phrase undoubtedly encompasses the conservation of natural resources, the maintenance of natural beauty, and the preservation of historic sites . . . .

Conservationists Can Have Legal Standing in Court

[The Federal Power Commission] argues that "petitioners do not have standing to obtain review" because they "make no claim of any personal economic injury resulting from the Commission's action."

Section 313(b) of the Federal Power Act, reads: "(b) Any party to a proceeding under this chapter aggrieved by an order issued by the Commission in such proceeding may obtain a review of such order in the United States Court of Appeals for any circuit wherein the licensee or public utility to which the order relates is located."

The Commission takes a narrow view of the meaning of "aggrieved party" under the Act. The Supreme Court has observed that the law of standing is a "complicated specialty of federal jurisdiction, the solution of whose problems is in any event more or less determined by the specific circumstances of individual situations." Although a "case" or "controversy" which is otherwise lacking cannot be created by statute, a statute may create new interests or rights and thus give standing to one who would otherwise be barred by the lack of a "case" or "controversy." The "case" or "controversy" requirement of Article III, § 2 of the Constitution does not require that an "aggrieved" or "adversely affected" party have a personal economic interest . . . .

In *State of Washington Dept. of Game v. Federal Power Comm.,* the Washington State Sportsmen's Council, Inc., a non-profit organization of residents, the State of Washington, Department of Game, and the State of Washington, Department of Fisheries, opposed the construction of a dam because it threatened to destroy fish. The Federal Power Commission granted the license; the intervenors applied for a rehearing which the Commission denied. Petitioners asked for review . . . and the court upheld their standing, noting: "All are 'parties aggrieved' since they claim that the Cowlitz Project will destroy fish in [sic] which they, among others, are interested in protecting."

The Federal Power Act seeks to protect non-economic as well as economic interests. Indeed, the Commission recognized this in framing the issue in this very case:

"The project is to be physically located in a general area of our nation steeped in the history of the American Revolution and of the colonial period. It is also a general area of great scenic beauty. The principal issue which must be decided is whether the project's effect on the scenic, historical and recreational values of the area are such that we should deny the application."

Protecting the Public Interest

In order to insure that the Federal Power Commission will adequately protect the public interest in the aesthetic, conservational, and recreational aspects of power development, those who by their activities and conduct have exhibited a special interest in such areas, must be held to be included in the class of "aggrieved" parties . . . . We hold that the Federal Power Act gives petitioners a legal right to protect their special interests . . . .

We see no justification for the Commission's fear that our determination will encourage "literally thousands" to intervene and seek review in future proceedings. We rejected a similar contention in *Associated Industries, Inc. v. Ickes,* (1943), noting that "no such horrendous possibilities" exist. Our experience with public actions confirms the view that the expense and vexation of legal proceedings is not lightly undertaken . . . .

Considering Both Private and Public Interests

Congress gave the Federal Power Commission a specific planning responsibility . . . . The totality of a project's immediate and long-range effects, and not merely the engineering and navigation aspects, are to be considered in a licensing proceeding . . . .

In this case, as in many others, the Commission has claimed to be the representative of the public interest. This role does not permit it to act as an umpire blandly calling balls and strikes for adversaries appearing before it; the right of the public must receive active and affirmative protection at the hands of the Commission.

This court cannot and should not attempt to substitute its judgment for that of the Commission. But we must decide whether the Commission has correctly discharged its duties, including the proper fulfillment of its planning function in deciding that the "licensing of the project would be in the overall public interest." The Commission must see to it that the record is complete. The Commission has an affirmative duty to inquire into and consider all relevant facts. . . .

The Commission should reexamine all questions on which we have found the record insufficient and all related matters. The Commission's renewed proceedings must include as a basic concern the preservation of natural beauty and of national historic shrines, keeping in mind that, in our affluent society, the cost of a project is only one of several factors to be considered. The record as it comes to us fails markedly to make out a case for the Storm King project on, among other matters, costs, public convenience and necessity, and absence of reasonable alternatives. Of course, the Commission should make every effort to expedite the new proceedings.

Petitioners' application, pursuant to Federal Power Act § 313(b), to adduce additional evidence concerning alternatives to the Storm King project and the cost and practicality of underground transmission facilities is granted.

The licensing order of March 9 and the two orders of May 6 are set aside, and the case remanded for further proceedings.

> *"Conflict, frequently sharp and bitter,*
> *has seemingly become an essential in-*
> *gredient . . . in arriving at decisions deal-*
> *ing with our environment."*

Conservation Must Be Balanced with Other Public Interests

Glenn Fowler

The following excerpt is taken from a New York Times *edito-*
rial written in 1969. Writer Glenn Fowler discusses the con-
flict over the construction of an electric power station at Storm
King Mountain on the Hudson River—a project that was
halted by a 1965 court decision in Scenic Hudson Preservation Conference v. Federal Power Commission. *He explains*
that while the Scenic Hudson Preservation Conference has
successfully fought construction of the Hudson River power
station, New York City does require increasing amounts of
electricity, and this necessitates the expansion of an existing
power station or the construction of a new one. According to
Fowler, the conflict over how to generate additional power il-
lustrates the challenge of balancing competing goods—in this
case the goals of increased power and environmental protec-
tion. He points out that whether the Consolidated Edison elec-
tric company builds a new plant along the Hudson River or
expands an existing plant in Queens, there will be some envi-
ronmental destruction.

Conflict, frequently sharp and bitter, has seemingly become
an essential ingredient in making decisions of public
policy. Nowhere is conflict more evident than in arriving at

Glenn Fowler, "Almost Any Policy Has Its Drawbacks," *The New York Times,* July
1969, p. R1. Copyright © 1969 by The New York Times Company. Reproduced by permission.

decisions dealing with our environment—the shape of our cities, the employment of our natural resources and the protection of our landscape, waterways and atmosphere from continued pollution.

In this arena, where we settle upon programs, expenditures and commitments that will determine the living climate in neighborhoods, whole cities and sometimes entire regions of the country for decades to come, there occurs a peculiar phenomenon. It is the conflict between two, and sometimes among several, courses of action each of which is generally acknowledged to be in the public good—but each of which has drawbacks that could outweigh the value of the proposed action.

A prime example of such a conflict situation occurred [in July 1969] when the Consolidated Edison Company said it planned to expand its oil-fueled power generating plant in the Astoria section of Queens. A simple decision to expand an existing power station would hardly seem to pose a difficult question of public policy, but in the context of the broader problem of how we propose to treat our environment, it takes on heavy overtones.

Increasing Power Needs

New York City is growing, if not in population at least in terms of power consumption within the five boroughs, as commerce and industry expand their facilities and families employ increasingly the fruits of a technological society. The capability to generate greater amounts of electric power each year must be acquired—indeed, for several years the generating capacity has barely been able to keep apace of peak demand, and only 10 days ago [on July 17, 1969] voluntary conservation was hurriedly invoked.

For several years Consolidated Edison and the city have been exploring ways to increase power-generating capacity.

The route that the utility now proposes to take—that of expanding the fossil-fuel Astoria power plant—is probably the least expensive, but it is the least desirable from another point of view. Consolidated Edison said two years ago that it would never again build an oil- or coal-burning plant in the metropolitan area, in order not to add to air pollution.

At one time plans were afoot to build an atomic-energy power plant in Queens, one that would have added no atmospheric pollutants and would have permitted closing of some existing fossil-fuel plants. But the idea of a nuclear-fuel plant in a crowded borough of the city precluded carrying out the scheme, even though it was never established whether the fears of radiation leakage or catastrophic explosion were real or imaginary.

The Proposed Storm King Plant

Consolidated Edison subsequently built a nuclear facility at Indian Point, N.Y., but it also sought to build a hydro-electric plant along the Hudson River on Storm King Mountain at Cornwall, N.Y., and this has been successfully fought by opponents for nearly a decade.

Conservationists are almost solidly united in opposition to the Storm King pumped-storage facility. They contend that it would be a blot on the landscape, would damage fish and other marine life in the Hudson and would pollute the river. The utility denies all this, and says it would employ exceptional safeguards to prevent any of these dire happenings. But the conservationists, bulwarked by an interstate compact set up to protect the river, have thus far prevailed.

A Conflict of Two "Good" Alternatives

Thus the conflict of "good" courses of action has come about. Consolidated Edison insists that New York City's power needs can best be met by the Storm King plant, which would obviate the need to expand the Astoria oil-burning plant that, even with the low-sulphur fuel that is to be used, will add to air pollution. The conservationist group, the Scenic Hudson Preservation Conference, asserts just as strongly that scarring the river life and landscape is no way to solve a shortage of power-generating capacity.

Can there be no compromise? In this case, probably not. Something is going to have to be hurt; no one has come up with an acceptable third course that would avoid both the damaging of Storm King and the expansion of the Astoria plant.

"The Storm King ... ruling remained the significant legal precedent, helping to establish the legitimacy of environmental issues."

Scenic Hudson Enabled the Emergence of Environmental Law

Natural Resources Defense Council

In the following viewpoint the Natural Resources Defense Council (NRDC) maintains that the Scenic Hudson *decision was a legal landmark that played a significant part in the development of environmental law. According to NRDC, that 1965 ruling established the legitimacy of environmental issues in the courts and the right of citizens to sue regulatory agencies and private companies for environmental harms. It also led to the creation of environmental public interest law firms that use legal means to gain environmental protection, explains the council, and spurred the passage of numerous laws protecting the environment. NRDC is a national environmental action organization that works to ensure a safe and healthy environment for all living things.*

Today there is a major branch of American jurisprudence whose practitioners meet their "clients" every time they step outdoors.

It may seem funny to think of forests and rivers and wetlands enjoying legal representation, but that is in essence what environmental public interest attorneys do: Use America's environmental statutes and legal precedents to advocate for and

Natural Resources Defense Council, "E-Law: What Started It All?" www.nrdc.org, May 5, 2000. Copyright © 2000 by the Natural Resources Defense Council. Reproduced by permission.

vigorously defend our natural resources. And they employ these same legal means in attempting to safeguard the public health from toxins and pollution.

Battleground at Storm King Mountain

It wasn't always this way. Environmental law has only been around since about the time of the first Earth Day in 1970. While its emergence can be traced to many large cultural and historical forces transforming the nation since World War II, the immediate cause was small enough: the announcement in 1963 by New York's utility company, Consolidated Edison, of plans to build a power plant on Storm King Mountain near the Hudson River. With the explosive growth of New York City and its suburbs, and the proliferation of home air conditioning and other major appliances, Con Ed wanted this plant to meet its customers' spiraling energy needs.

Though many residents of the nearby town of Cornwall-on-Hudson wanted the Con Ed plant because it would mean jobs and a boost to the local economy, a few longtime residents of the area—led by Wall Street lawyer Stephen Duggan and his wife Beatrice "Smokey" Duggan—launched a campaign to halt it. Storm King Mountain, the surrounding Hudson Highlands, and indeed the entire Hudson River Valley, held a special place in American culture as the distinctively American wilderness venerated by the nation's earliest writers such as James Fenimore Cooper, Nathaniel Hawthorne, and Washington Irving, as well as the Hudson River school of landscape artists, including Thomas Cole, Asher Durand, and Frederick Church. The Duggans believed their beloved Hudson Highlands were as beautiful as anything in the Rhine Valley in Germany, and worth fighting to preserve.

At first they managed to attract only a few supporters. But when Con Ed made the mistake of publishing a drawing that actually exaggerated the size of the plant relative to its surroundings, the Duggans' phone began to ring with offers of support. Soon, the Duggans and the other Cornwall landowners were joined by various New York hikers' groups and conservationists in opposing the Con Ed plant. They called themselves the Scenic Hudson Preservation Conference.

The struggle, at first, was very much tilted in Con Edison's favor. The issues before the Federal Power Commission (FPC), which would grant Con Ed the right to proceed after public hearings, were largely technical in nature: Was the plant needed? Was Con Ed capable of building and operating it? And so on. Aesthetic considerations were irrelevant. At a hearing convened by the FPC the judge ruled in favor of Con Ed, despite Scenic Hudson's testimony that the plant's construction would mar one of the nation's scenic and cultural treasures. Scenic Hudson attorney Lloyd Garrison, a descendant of the famed 19th-century Boston abolitionist William Lloyd Garrison, immediately appealed the Commission's decision, sending the matter to a federal circuit court.

A Landmark Decision

There was little precedent for the federal judiciary to overrule decisions made by regulatory agencies like the FPC, and judges were traditionally reluctant to involve themselves in technical matters outside their expertise. But Garrison did not engage them on technical points; instead he argued, in *Scenic Hudson Preservation Conference v. Federal Power Commission* (1965), that the FPC had failed to protect the public interest in accordance with its Congressional mandate under the Federal Power Act (1920), by not adequately considering all the factors that were of interest to the public, namely, the beauty and historical significance of Storm King Mountain.

At the circuit court hearing Garrison was quiet but passionate, while the Con Ed attorney Randall LeBoeuf offended the judge with a show of arrogance, at one point even referring to the Scenic Hudson lawyers as "birdwatchers." When

LeBoeuf stated that the plant Con Ed had designed would actually improve the beauty of Storm King Mountain, the court was incredulous. On December 29, 1965, it ruled in favor of Scenic Hudson, setting aside Con Ed's license and ordering the FPC to hold new hearings. Scenic Hudson, the court ruled, had "standing to sue" in the case.

The decision was a legal landmark. For the first time, a conservation group had been permitted to sue to protect the public interest. Although Scenic Hudson had no economic interest in Storm King—the usual basis for standing—the court ruled that it nonetheless could be construed to be an "injured party" and was entitled to judicial review of an agency ruling.

The Storm King battle would be fought for another decade before Con Edison was finally forced to abandon plans for the plant, but the 1965 ruling remained the significant legal precedent, helping to establish the legitimacy of environmental issues and opening the way for lawyers and the courts to play a highly significant role in all manner of land-use and environmental battles.

First Environmental Laws

Perhaps the leading model for would-be environmental public interest attorneys during this period was the NAACP [National Association for the Advancement of Colored People] Legal Defense and Educational Fund, which pioneered the idea of using test cases—specific examples of racial injustice—to illustrate the larger inequity of race relations in America, and to establish useful legal precedents for bringing needed reforms. The NAACP had won a series of historic cases, including *Brown v. Board of Education* (1954), which had struck down the "separate but equal" doctrine that had allowed segregation in schools until then.

But while the NAACP had the equal rights provision of the 14th Amendment on which to base its cases, environmen-

31

tal lawyers had nothing comparable. Applicable statutes were few, and principles of common law—including nuisance, trespass, and strict liability—were difficult to apply because they had evolved to protect individual property rather than broad public interests.

This state of affairs soon changed. As the decade drew to a close, environmental concerns that had been building throughout the 1960s swept to the top of the nation's political agenda, and on New Years Day, 1970, President [Richard] Nixon signed into law the National Environmental Policy Act (NEPA). Among other things, it required that federal agencies conduct thorough assessments of the environmental impact of all major programs. (This provision, duplicated ultimately at state and local levels across America, remains a cornerstone of environmental law.)

Then came Earth Day, April 22, 1970, when massive rallies took place on virtually every college campus in America and in most large cities. TV and magazines gave the events extensive coverage, and both houses of Congress stood in recess in honor of the occasion.

With the president's basic approval, and public opinion loudly and clearly expressed by the Earth Day demonstrations, legislators in Washington and in state capitols and city halls across the nation in the early 1970s passed thousands of new environmental laws and ordinances. At the federal level, in addition to NEPA, the most important laws were the 1970 amendments to several pieces of "clean air" legislation dating back to 1963 (laws that collectively became known as the Clean Air Act), and the Federal Water Pollution Control Act of 1972, commonly known as the Clean Water Act. From these laws there evolved a large body of environmental case law. Subsequent federal legislation, notably the Consumer Product Safety Act (1972), the Environmental Pesticide Control Act (1972), the Endangered Species Act (1973), the Safe Drinking Water Act (1974), the Toxic Substances Control Act

(1976), the Superfund legislation to clean up hazardous waste sites (1980), and the Emergency Planning and Community Right-to-Know Act (1986) added to the rising edifice of environmental statutes, and the lawyers who filed cases citing these laws created a huge annex of legal precedents.

Environmental lawyers who prior to 1970 had worried about the barrenness of their legal arsenal now found themselves armed with an abundance of new statutory weapons. The challenge was no longer to adapt principles of common law to environmental issues or dust off old, little-used statutes, but rather to monitor the administration of new statutes by the Environmental Protection Agency (EPA), itself a creation of the Nixon administration, and when necessary to prod the agency and test the laws by filing lawsuits.

Putting the Laws to Work

Two key environmental public interest law firms emerged from this productive period. The Environmental Defense Fund (EDF) was formed in 1967 as an outgrowth of a lawsuit brought by Long Island citizens to restrain the use of DDT [insecticide] by the Suffolk County Mosquito Control Commission. The Natural Resources Defense Council (NRDC) started in 1970 as the result of a partnership between a group of young, idealistic Yale Law School students and the older New York "establishment" attorneys of the Scenic Hudson Preservation Conference, led by Stephen Duggan, who had already incorporated under the NRDC name.

Since then, environmental lawyers have achieved great strides for the environment by using the legal means at their disposal to clean up rivers, decrease air pollution, ban toxic substances, force government and industry to comply with regulations, and even to prod the U.S. to participate in international negotiations on global climate change issues. And environmental law is so firmly established, it is taught as a separate branch of legal studies at most law schools today.

| "Our courts have ... thrust needless obstacles before environmental litigants."

The Benefits of *Scenic Hudson* Have Been Short-Lived

Philip Weinberg

While Scenic Hudson *was a landmark decision that established the right of conservationists to file environmental lawsuits, that right has since been greatly eroded by the courts, argues Philip Weinberg in the following viewpoint. In Weinberg's opinion, a number of recent Supreme Court decisions have severely limited the right of private parties to sue the government or businesses for environmental abuses. He believes the United States should follow the example of other countries such as the Philippines and Pakistan, where the courts recognize that in order to prevent government abuses of power, citizens must have the right to legally fight to protect their environment. Weinberg is a professor of law at St. John's University School of Law, New York, and author of* Environmental Law: Cases and Materials.

Environmental protection in the United States has in large measure been achieved through the courts. The signal victories as early as the 1960s were judicial—most tellingly, the halting of the power project that would have defaced Storm King Mountain in New York's Hudson Highlands [in 1965] and the Interstate highway that would have destroyed the integrity of Memphis's Overton Park [in 1971]. These decisions were of first magnitude in themselves as well as for the precedents they established for future suits. They directly led to the numerous actions brought by concerned citizens and environ-

Philip Weinberg, "Local Environmental Laws: Forging a New Weapon in Environmental Protection," *Pace Environmental Law Review,* vol. 89, 2003. Copyright © 2003 by *Pace Environmental Law Review.* Reproduced by permission.

mental advocacy organizations to review adverse governmental decisions and enjoin harmful activities. Without such recourse in the courts there would be scant leverage to overturn government actions, no matter how damaging to the environment they might be.

Unlike most other litigation, the issue of the plaintiffs' standing to bring the suit is often a major one in environmental suits brought by private parties—as is also the case in suits involving civil liberties and constitutional issues. . . .

The Expansion of Standing in the Federal Courts

The 1960s and 1970s saw citizen standing expanded in the federal courts, both in environmental and constitutional litigation. The harbinger of increased citizen standing was *Scenic Hudson Preservation Conference v. Federal Power Commission,* in which the Second Circuit roundly rebuffed challenges to the standing of litigants seeking court review of the license issued to construct a pumped-storage hydroelectric plant atop Storm King Mountain in the Hudson Highlands. The court held the petitioners, conservation groups, their members, and neighboring towns, were "aggrieved" parties under the Federal Power Act, and had standing to obtain judicial review of the Commission's licensing decision. As it noted,

> In order to insure that the . . . Commission will . . . protect the public interest in the aesthetic, conservational, and recreational aspects of power development, those who by their activities and conduct have exhibited a special interest in such areas, must be held to be included in the class of "aggrieved" parties under [the Act] . . . .

The Clean Air Act was the first federal environmental regulatory statute to contain a citizen-suit provision. . . . Designed to finesse the standing disputes that had delayed or hamstrung plaintiffs in environmental litigation, this statute provides that "any person may commence a civil action" in federal district court to enjoin violations of emission standards or limitations, as well as enforcement orders and certain types of permit violations. Plaintiffs must give sixty days' notice to the EPA [Environmental Protection Agency], the state and the alleged violator . . . .

The citizen suit provision has in fact widened access to the courts in air-quality cases. The courts have generously construed it. In one notable and enlightened decision, *Friends of the Earth v. Carey,* the court sustained a citizen suit and enjoined violations of a State Implementation Plan adopted by New York pursuant to the Clean Air Act, noting that "in enacting [the citizen-suit provision], Congress made clear that citizen groups are not to be treated as nuisances or troublemakers but rather as welcomed participants in the vindication of environmental interests . . . . Thus the Act seeks to encourage citizen participation rather than treat it as a curiosity or a theoretical remedy." Quoting an earlier case, the court noted: "Fearing that administrative enforcement might falter or stall, 'the citizen suits provision reflected a deliberate choice by Congress to widen citizen access to the courts, as a supplemental and effective assurance that the Act would be implemented and enforced.'" . . .

This pattern continued with the enactment of citizen suit provisions in the Clean Water Act, Endangered Species Act, Resource Conservation and Recovery Act, and Comprehensive Environmental Response, Compensation and Liability Act (CERCLA), the last two of which have proved to be a foundation for numerous suits to compel cleanup of hazardous waste sites . . . .

The Assault on Standing

In a series of decisions in the 1990s, the Supreme Court first cabined, then actively sought to truncate, standing in environmental litigation . . . .

Justice [Antonin] Scalia fired the opening salvo in *Lujan v. National Wildlife Federation.* The suit was brought to challenge actions of the Secretary of the Interior taken under the Federal Land Policy and Management Act (FLPMA), which authorizes the Department of the Interior to review withdrawals of government-owned land from mining and similar commercial uses. The National Wildlife Federation (NWF), a respected conservation group, and several of its members, contended the cancellation of some of these withdrawals was done in violation of the FLPMA by failing to adopt land-use plans, and without the environmental impact review contemplated by NEPA [National Environmental Policy Act].

The Court ruled the plaintiffs were not "aggrieved" as required by the Administrative Procedure Act. Although they were within the zone of interests of the FLPMA, which the Court agreed the Act was written to protect, the affidavits of the two members of the NWF submitted to show standing were, it ruled, too broad to satisfy the requirement of particular injury. The affidavits referred to areas of millions of acres, of which only a few thousand were being removed from the Act's protection. As the district court had concluded, "there is no showing that [the plaintiff's] recreational use and enjoyment extends to the particular 4,500 acres covered by the decision to terminate classification to the remainder of the two million acres affected by the termination." . . .

Just two years later, the Court, in *Lujan v. Defenders of Wildlife,* took an even greater swipe at standing, this time undeterred by a citizen-suit statute. The suit challenged a Department of the Interior regulation limiting to United States territory the applicability of the Endangered Species Act provision requiring federal agencies to consult with the Department to "insure that any action authorized, funded or carried out by such agency . . . is not likely to jeopardize the continued existence of any endangered species or threatened species or result in the destruction . . . of [its critical] habitat. . . ."

The plaintiff conservation group and its members contended the new rule, which replaced a rule applying the statute to federally funded or performed actions worldwide, contradicted the statute, which contained no geographic limits, and the lower court had so held.

Justice Scalia again wrote for the Court. He noted that Article III [of the U.S. Constitution] standing requires injury in fact, traceable to the defendant's actions, and likely ("as opposed to merely 'speculative'") to be redressable by the court. He went on to emphasize that these "are not mere pleading requirements but rather an indispensable part of the plaintiff's case," and must be supported with evidence. And here, the Court concluded, the plaintiff failed to show "injury in fact." Affidavits by two members of Defenders asserted that they were wildlife biologists interested professionally in endangered or threatened species—the Nile crocodile, the Asian elephant and leopard—whose critical habitat was at risk through United States funded construction projects: a dam in Egypt and a development project in Sri Lanka. The members alleged that they had visited those sites and intended to return to study those species, but were concerned lest their habitat be damaged before then. But, the Court found, "'some day' intentions [to return] do not support a finding of the 'actual or imminent' injury that our cases require." In short, a plaintiff must "show that he will soon expose himself to the injury." It went on to reject the plaintiffs' further claim that as zoologists they had sufficient interest in these species' habitat to confer standing, coolly observing that

> Under these theories, anyone who goes to see Asian elephants in the Bronx Zoo, and anyone who is a keeper of Asian elephants in the Bronx Zoo, has standing to sue because the Director of the Agency for International Development (AID) did not consult with the Secretary regarding the AID-funded project in Sri Lanka. This is beyond all reason. . . .

Defenders was clearly designed to impose barriers to standing despite the plain intent of Congress in enacting citizen-suit legislation. The assault appeared likely to succeed. In fact, the Court's next significant decision on standing in environmental suits extended *Defenders* somewhat, relying heavily on the redressability argument that had failed to convince a majority in *Defenders*.

Steel Co. v. Citizens for a Better Environment [1998] also involved a citizen suit, this time, in contrast to *Defenders*, against a company that had concededly and blatantly violated environmental laws designed to safeguard public health. The defendant had for eight successive years failed to submit reports of its storage and release of hazardous chemicals as required by the Emergency Planning and Community Right-to-Know Act (EPCRA). Once it received the required 60-day notice of impending citizen suit, however, the company hastily filed the required reports. Again leading the charge, Justice Scalia concluded this belated compliance went beyond rendering the action moot, and actually deprived the plaintiff of standing to commence the suit . . . .

Standing in Other Nations' Environmental Litigation

It is somewhat ironic that the highest courts of three developing countries far from our shores, all with legal systems based on Anglo-American principles, have ruled that plaintiffs have standing in environmental litigation without having to negotiate the barriers imposed by American courts. We have much to learn from these recent decisions rendered by Asian courts.

The Philippines' highest court, in *Oposa v. Factoran* [1993], upheld the standing of minors and the Philippine Ecological Network, Inc. to sue to cancel licenses to extract timber from that country's pristine rainforest. The action was based on a constitutional provision that "the State shall protect and advance the right of the people to a balanced and healthful ecology." The court ruled the minor plaintiffs could sue on their own behalf as well as for future generations, since "the minors' assertion of their right to sound environment constitutes, at the same time, the performance of [the defendants'] obligation to ensure the protection of that right for the generations to come . . . ."

Pakistan's Supreme Court likewise held in *Zia v. WAPDA* (Water and Power Development Authority) [1994] that citizens had standing to sue to enjoin construction of a power transmission grid without alleging special or individual injury, because of asserted health concerns from electromagnetic fields. This suit was based on that nation's due process clause, which reads similarly to our own. The court held that:

> Where life of citizens is degraded, the quality of life is adversely affected and health hazards are created affecting a large number of people the court in exercise of its jurisdiction under Article 184(3) of the Constitution may grant relief to the extent of stopping the functioning of units which create pollution and environmental degradation.

That article empowers the Pakistani Supreme Court to issue orders to enforce the fundamental rights, including due process rights, enumerated earlier in the constitution.

Similarly, the High Court Division of Bangladesh ruled in *Farooque v. Bangladesh* [1997] that the Bangladesh Environmental Lawyers' Association could challenge the lack of environmental impact assessments for several development projects. The court specifically noted that "if a fundamental right is involved, the impugned matter need not affect a purely personal right of the applicant touching him alone. It is enough if he shares that right in common with others."

Needless Obstacles Imposed on Conservationists

Our courts have abused the historic rules of standing and thrust needless obstacles before environmental litigants. . . .

This issue is not just one of procedural niceties or judicial economy. Limiting standing in environmental litigation gives government agencies and industry carte blanche to violate laws enacted to safeguard public health and protect natural resources. For all the pieties mouthed about the need to ensure the separation of powers the true separation of powers concern is the need for the courts, as always, to curb abuses by the other two branches, a need voiced as early as *Marbury v. Madison* [1803] and many times since. It is still, as was true two centuries ago, "emphatically the province and duty of the judicial department to say what the law is." This can only happen if litigants are free, within reasonable and historic limits, to enter the courthouse.

CHAPTER 2

Balancing Wildlife Management Against Economic Interests

Case Overview

Seattle Audubon Society v. John L. Evans and Washington Contract Loggers Association (1991)

The Pacific Northwest is home to a significant portion of the United States' federally owned forests. These forests provide an essential habitat for thousands of plants and animal species and support recreation and tourism in that area. At the same time, however, the forests are also vital to the timber industry, which provides wood for lumber and wood products and affords a livelihood for thousands of people. The management of these forests, like that of many of America's other natural resources, requires balancing the protection of natural resources with the protection of economic needs. In the later 1900s a conflict over the northern spotted owl, a small bird that resides in Pacific Northwest forests, illustrated how complex the process of wildlife management is and how high the stakes are for everyone involved. *Seattle Audubon Society v. John L. Evans and Washington Contract Loggers Association* was one of a number of lawsuits filed in the 1990s over the protection of the spotted owl. It epitomized the ongoing difficulty America faces as it attempts to create a viable balance between economic needs and the preservation of the natural environment.

The northern spotted owl lives primarily in old-growth forests—those that contain very old trees that have not been harvested regularly. Beginning in the late 1960s, numerous studies showed that the owl population was shrinking as a result of logging in these forests. In 1990 the Fish and Wildlife Service listed the owl as threatened with extinction. The next year the Seattle Audubon Society, a conservation organization, sued the Forest Service (represented by John L. Evans) and the Washington Contract Loggers Association to stop the sale of

Marianne Jewell Memorial Library
Baker College of Muskegon
Muskegon, Michigan 49442

logging rights in spotted owl habitats in national forests until the Forest Service took actions to ensure the protection of the owl.

The Seattle Audubon Society and other environmentalists opposed to logging in the area argued that old-growth forests were critical to forest ecology and the survival of certain species, including the spotted owl. They charged that in managing these forests, the Forest Service was acting solely in the interests of the timber industry. If logging were allowed to continue at the same pace, they feared, unique ecosystems and species would be destroyed.

In 1991 the harvesting of trees was a dominant economic force throughout the Pacific Northwest, however, and the timber industry insisted that to halt logging in spotted owl habitat would virtually end logging and devastate the economy of that region. It argued that habitat preservation must be balanced with the protection of jobs and that in this case the protection of the owl was not important enough to destroy an entire industry. In 1989 the president of the Northwest Forestry Association summed up this belief when he stated, "To devastate a regional economy over the spotted owl seems absurd. You're talking about affecting half our industry."

In 1991 the U.S. District Court for the Western District of Washington ruled otherwise. It decided that the spotted owl was worthy of protection and that the Forest Service must halt logging until it adopted standards and guidelines to ensure a viable population of spotted owls was maintained in the forests. As a result of the 1991 decision, the Forest Service adopted the Northwest Forest Plan in 1994, which reduced logging by more than 80 percent to protect habitat for species such as the spotted owl. However, both sides complain that this solution has been unsatisfactory. Timber companies continue to protest the loss of revenue and jobs and press for changes to the Northwest Forest Plan and other regulations to allow more logging. At the same time, environmentalists point out that the reduction in logging may not have been enough and that the northern spotted owl and other species in that area continue to decline. According to a study conducted by a private firm for the Fish and Wildlife Service, overall, northern spotted owls declined by about 3.7 percent per year from 1985 to 2003.

Seattle Audubon illustrates the difficulty of making choices about wildlife management. In most cases, as in that of the spotted owl, there are compelling arguments for both conservation and industrial use of natural resources. Thus, the Forest Service and other government agencies that manage America's natural resources must continually balance economic needs with conservation.

"The Forest Service is ... charged with managing ... [land] 'in a way that maximizes long term net public benefit in an environmentally sound manner.'"

The Court's Decision: Wildlife Conservation and Economic Health Can Coexist

William L. Dwyer

The following viewpoint is excerpted from Judge William L. Dwyer's May 23, 1991, ruling in Seattle Audubon Society v. John L. Evans and Washington Contract Loggers Association, *decided in the U.S. District Court for the Western District of Washington. In response to disagreement over whether logging should be allowed in northern spotted owl habitat, Dwyer rules that the Forest Service must halt logging until it adopts standards and guidelines that will ensure that a viable population of owls is maintained in the forests. According to Dwyer, the responsibility of the Forest Service is to balance economic interests with conservation. In this case, he argues, research shows that the spotted owl and the old growth forest it lives in are endangered, yet the Forest Service has not taken action to protect the owl or the forests. In his opinion, while halting logging may have undesirable economic and social consequences, the potential loss of forests is a far greater tragedy. Dwyer served as a U.S. district court judge from 1987 until his death in 2002.*

O n March 7, 1991, the court entered an order on summary judgment declaring unlawful a proposal of defen-

William L. Dwyer, opinion, *Seattle Audubon Society v. John L. Evans and Washington Contract Loggers Association,* 771 F. Supp. 1081, May 23, 1991.

dants John L. Evans, et al. (collectively the "Forest Service") to log northern spotted owl habitat in national forests located in Washington, Oregon, and Northern California without complying with requirements of the National Forest Management Act ("NFMA"). On the basis of that order plaintiffs Seattle Audubon Society, et al. (collectively "SAS") have moved for a permanent injunction prohibiting the sale of logging rights in additional spotted owl habitat areas until the Forest Service complies with NFMA and its regulations by adopting standards and guidelines to assure that a viable population of the species is maintained in the forests. The Forest Service proposes a different injunction, one that would permit, in the interim, additional sales in owl habitat if they are consistent with the recommendations of the Report of the Interagency Scientific Committee to Address the Conservation of the Northern Spotted Owl ("ISC Report") issued in April 1990. Intervenors Washington Contract Loggers Association, et al. (collectively "WCLA") support the Forest Service's proposal. The two sides agree that the court should set a date for the Forest Service to adopt a plan to assure the owl's viability . . . .

Maintaining Viable Populations

The national forests are managed by the Forest Service under NFMA. Regulations promulgated under that statute provide that

> fish and wildlife shall be managed to maintain viable populations of existing native and desired non-native vertebrate species in the planning area.

[According to the statute] a viable population is "one which has the estimated numbers and distribution of reproductive individuals to insure its continued existence is well distributed in the planning area." To insure viability, habitat must be provided to support at least a minimum number of reproductive individuals.

Since not every species can be monitored, "indicator species" are observed as signs of general wildlife viability. The northern spotted owl is an indicator species.

While having these conservation duties, the Forest Service is also charged with managing these lands to "provide for multiple use and sustained yield of goods and services from the National Forest System in a way that maximizes long term net public benefit in an environmentally sound manner."

In recent years logging and development have steadily reduced wildlife habitat in the Pacific Northwest. At the same time many local mills have experienced log shortages. The result is an intensified struggle over the future of the national forests . . . .

[An] evidentiary hearing held from April 30 to May 9, 1991, provided a wealth of information. Expert testimony of high quality from biologists, economists, and others was presented by both sides. From the evidence admitted at the hearing the court makes and enters the following findings of fact:

Background Findings

1. The fate of the spotted owl has become a battleground largely because the species is a symbol of the remaining old growth forest. As stated in the ISC Report:

> Why all the fuss about the status and welfare of this particular bird? The numbers, distribution, and welfare of spotted owls are widely believed to be inextricably tied to mature and old-growth forests. Such forests have been significantly reduced since 1850 (mostly since 1950) by clearing for agriculture, urban development, natural events such as fire and windstorms, and most significantly, by logging in recent decades. Nearly all old growth has been removed on private lands. Most of the remainder is under the management of the BLM [Bureau of Land Management], FS [Forest Service], and NPS [National Park Service] on Federal lands. As its habitat has declined, the owl has virtually disappeared from some areas and its numbers are decreasing in others.

2. An old growth forest consists not just of ancient standing trees, but of fallen trees, snags, massive decaying vegetation, and numerous resident plant and animal species, many of which live nowhere else.

3. A great conifer forest originally covered the western parts of Washington, Oregon, and Northern California, from the Cascade and Coast mountains to the sea. Perhaps ten percent of it remains. The spaces protected as parks or wilderness areas are not enough for the survival of the northern spotted owl.

4. The old growth forest sustains a biological community far richer than those of managed forests or tree farms. As testified by Dr. William Ferrell, a forest ecologist:

The most significant implication from our new knowledge regarding old-growth forest ecology is that logging these forests destroys not just trees, but a complex, distinctive, and unique ecosystem.

5. The remaining old growth stands are valued also for their effects on climate, air, and migratory fish runs, and for their beauty. A 1984 Forest Service document summed up the controversy:

There are at least three main reasons cited for maintaining old growth: wildlife and plant habitat, ecosystem diversity, and preservation of aesthetic qualities. Those opposed to the retention of old growth are primarily concerned with economic factors and urge rapid conversion of the existing old growth to managed forests of productive, young age classes.

6. Through most of the country's history there was little or no logging in the national forests. Intensive logging began with World War II and has accelerated.

7. NFMA was adopted in 1976, after three decades of heavy logging, in the hope of serving both wilderness and industry

In 1991 the Supreme Court ruled to temporarily halt logging in old-growth forests in order to protect the habitat of the endangered northern spotted owl. © Corel Corporation

values. Senator [Hubert] Humphrey of Minnesota, a sponsor of the act, stated:

> The days have ended when the forest may be viewed only as trees and trees viewed only as timber. The soil and the water, the grasses and the shrubs, the fish and the wildlife, and the beauty that is the forest must become integral parts of resource managers' thinking and actions.

8. Despite increasing concern over the environment, logging sales by the Forest Service have continued on a large scale. Timber harvests in the national forests in Washington and Oregon ranged from 4.448 billion to 5.082 billion board feet per year in 1985 through 1989, amounting to between 30% and 33% of the total harvested in those states in those years.

9. Some major firms in the Pacific Northwest have extensive private forests and need little or no wood from public

sources. Many small mills and logging companies depend in whole or in part on federal timber.

10. Mill owners and loggers, and their employees, especially in small towns, have developed since World War II an expectation that federal timber will be available indefinitely, and a way of life that cannot be duplicated elsewhere.

11. The region's timber industry has been going through fundamental changes. The most important is modernization which increases productivity and reduces the demand for labor (i.e., the jobs available). There have also been recent changes in product demand, in competition from other parts of the country and the world, and in the export of raw logs for processing in the Far East. The painful results for many workers, and their families and communities, will continue regardless of whether owl habitat in the national forests is protected.

Statutory Violations

12. The records of this case . . . show a remarkable series of violations of the environmental laws. The Forest Service defended its December 1988 ROD[1] persistently for nearly two years. . . . But in the fall of 1990 the Forest Service admitted that the ROD was inadequate after all—that it would fail to preserve the northern spotted owl. In seeking a stay of proceedings in this court in 1989 the Forest Service announced its intent to adopt temporary guidelines within thirty days. It did not do that within thirty days, or ever. When directed by Congress to have a revised ROD in place by September 30, 1990, the Forest Service did not even attempt to comply. The FWS [Fish and Wildlife Service], in the meantime, acted contrary to law in refusing to list the spotted owl as endangered or threatened. After it finally listed the species as "threatened" following Judge [Thomas] Zilly's order [in 1991], the FWS

1. In December 1988 the Forest Service issued a Record of Decision (ROD) outlining standards and guidelines for managing northern spotted owl habitat in national forests.

again violated the ESA [Endangered Species Act] by failing to designate critical habitat as required. Another order had to be issued setting a deadline for the FWS to comply with the law.

13. The reasons for this pattern of behavior were made clear at the evidentiary hearing.

Dr. Eric Forsman, a research wildlife biologist with the Forest Service, testified, in regard to the 1988 ROD and other Forest Service plans for the spotted owl that preceded the ISC Report:

> Q. Were you satisfied at the time with the results of those previous works?
>
> A. No. On all of those plans, I had considerable reservations for a variety of reasons. But primarily because in every instance, there was a considerable—I would emphasize considerable—amount of political pressure to create a plan which was an absolute minimum. That is, which had a very low probability of success and which had a minimum impact on timber harvest. . . .

Probability of Irreparable Harm

22. The northern spotted owl is now threatened with extinction. The ISC Report states:

> We have concluded that the owl is imperiled over significant portions of its range because of continuing losses of habitat from logging and natural disturbances. Current management strategies are inadequate to ensure its viability. Moreover, in some portions of the owl's range, few options for managing habitat remain open, and available alternatives are steadily declining throughout the bird's range. For these reasons, delay in implementing a conservation strategy cannot be justified on the basis of inadequate knowledge. . . .

Economic and Social Consequences

44. Over the past decade many timber jobs have been lost and mills closed in the Pacific Northwest. The main reasons

have been modernization of physical plants, changes in product demand, and competition from elsewhere. Supply shortages have also played a part. Those least able to adapt and modernize, and those who have not gained alternative supplies, have been hardest hit by the changes. By and large, the companies with major capital resources and private timber supplies have done well; many of the smaller firms have had trouble.

45. Job losses in the wood products industry will continue regardless of whether the northern spotted owl is protected. A credible estimate is that over the next twenty years more than 30,000 jobs will be lost to worker-productivity increases alone.

46. A social cost is paid whenever an economic transformation of this nature takes place, all the more so when a largely rural industry loses sizeable numbers of jobs. Today, however, in contrast to earlier recession periods, states offer programs for dislocated workers that ease and facilitate the necessary adjustments. . . .

48. The timber industry no longer drives the Pacific Northwest's economy. In Oregon, for example, the level of employment in lumber and wood products declined by seventeen percent between 1979 and 1989. In the same period, Oregon's total employment increased by twenty-three percent.

49. The wood products industry now employs about four percent of all workers in Western Oregon, two percent in Western Washington, and six percent in Northern California. Even if some jobs in wood products were affected by protecting owl habitat in the short term, any effect on the regional economy probably would be small.

50. The remaining wilderness contributes to the desirability of this region as a site for new industries and their employees. The resulting economic gains, while hard to measure, are genuine and substantial. The FWS has recently noted that preservation of old growth brings economic benefits and amenities "of extremely high value."

The Public Interest and the Balance of Equities

The court must weigh and consider the public interest in deciding whether to issue an injunction in an environmental case. It must also consider the balance of equities among the parties.

The problem here has not been any shortcoming in the laws, but simply a refusal of administrative agencies to comply with them. . . . This invokes a public interest of the highest order: the interest in having government officials act in accordance with law.

The public also "has a manifest interest in the preservation of old growth trees." [*Pilchuck Audubon Soc'y v. MacWilliams,* 1998.]

This is not the usual situation in which the court reviews an administrative decision and, in doing so, gives deference to agency expertise. The Forest Service here has not taken the necessary steps to make a decision in the first place—yet it seeks to take action with major environmental impact.

The loss of an additional 66,000 acres of spotted owl habitat, without a conservation plan being in place, and with no agency having committed itself to the ISC strategy, would constitute irreparable harm, and would risk pushing the species beyond a threshold from which it could not recover.

Any reduction in federal timber sales will have adverse effects on some timber industry firms and their employees, and a suspension of owl habitat sales in the national forests is no exception. But while the loss of old growth is permanent, the economic effects of an injunction [on logging] are temporary and can be minimized in many ways . . . .

To bypass the environmental laws, either briefly or permanently, would not fend off the changes transforming the timber industry. The argument that the mightiest economy on earth cannot afford to preserve old growth forests for a short time, while it reaches an overdue decision on how to manage them, is not convincing today. It would be even less so a year or a century from now.

For the reasons stated, the public interest and the balance of equities require the issuance of an injunction directing the Forest Service to comply with the requirements of NFMA by March 5, 1992, and preventing it from selling additional logging rights in spotted owl habitat until it complies with the law.

> "The illusion of a pending owl extinction
> is a parable of modern environmental-
> ism, illustrating . . . the internal faults
> that . . . could bring it down."

Seattle Audubon Reveals the Environmentalists' Flawed Tactics

Gregg Easterbrook

*In order to halt the logging of old-growth forests in Oregon, en-
vironmentalists have falsely spread claims about a pending owl
extinction there, argues Gregg Easterbrook in the following viewpoint. He contends that spotted owl numbers are far higher than
environmentalists claim and that the bird is not in danger of extinction. Easterbrook believes that old-growth forests do need to
be preserved; however, he maintains that environmentalists
should not exaggerate the threat to owls in their attempt to halt
logging. Such a tactic will harm the credibility and effectiveness
of the environmental movement, he maintains. Instead he advocates honesty about the owls as the best way to preserve both forests and jobs. Gregg Easterbrook is a senior editor of the* New
Republic, *a contributing editor of the* Atlantic Monthly, *and a
visiting fellow at the Brookings Institution.*

Recently, I rather casually did something that according to
contemporary environmental orthodoxy is inconceivable:
I took a hike through the woods and saw lots of spotted owls.
Spotted owls are said to be so rare that even an experienced
forester spends weeks trying to glimpse one. I saw four in a

Gregg Easterbrook, "The Birds—the Spotted Owl: An Environmental Parable," *The
New Republic,* vol. 210, March 28, 1994, p. 22. Copyright © 1994 by The New Republic, Inc. Reproduced by permission.

few hours. The owls were living wild in a habitat where it is presumed impossible for them to exist: a young woodland, not an old-growth forest. And they were living in a place, California, where environmental doctrine holds spotted owls to be rare birds indeed.

In the evolution of political issues there often comes a sequence that runs like this: A new concern arises. For a while the system attempts to deny the claim's validity, but eventually some action is taken. By then advocates have become an interest group, fighting as much for the preservation of their cause as anything else. The fight takes on a life of its own; the specifics of the original issue are discarded.

Claims About Owl Extinction

Today [in 1994] this sequence may be repeating in the matter of the spotted owl. A decade ago researchers warned that the bird was declining toward extinction. Legal gears were set spinning. In 1991 a federal judge suspended most Northwest logging, resulting in the loss of thousands of high-wage jobs. This month [March 1994] the [Bill] Clinton administration is set to file court documents that make most of those losses permanent.[1] The Clinton owl plan has become a standard Washington lobbying jangle in which business and environmental constituencies drop sixteen-ton weights on each others' heads. The original question of whether the owl is endangered has been discarded. At the White House level, that isn't even discussed anymore. Political and legal maneuvers continue on the assumption that 1980s studies hypothesizing an owl extinction were correct.

They may not be. Research is beginning to suggest that the spotted owl exists in numbers far greater than was assumed when the extinction alarm sounded. Whereas a headline-making 1986 Audubon Society report said that 1,500 spotted

1. The Northwest Forest Plan, adopted in 1994, reduced logging by more than 80 percent to protect habitat for species such as the spotted owl.

owl pairs throughout the United States was the number necessary to prevent extinction, it now seems that as many as 10,000
pairs may exist. "It appears the spotted owl population is not
in as bad a shape as imagined ten years ago, or even five years
ago," says David Wilcove, a biodiversity expert for the Environmental Defense Fund. Thus Clinton's plan to shut down
most Washington and Oregon logging may not only be un-
necessary; it may be resting on an illusion.

The illusion of a pending owl extinction is a parable of
modern environmentalism, illustrating both its manifest virtues and the internal faults that, uncorrected, could bring it
down. The owl fixation has its political virtues: it's an issue
easily understood by the public; it graphically illustrates the
genuine need for old-growth forest preservation; and it has allowed environmentalism to win numerous battles against the
government and the logging industry. Also, as a direct-mail
fund-raising tool, the little feathered creature cannot be beat;
as a symbol of endangered species, the owl can help protect
many others that are not so cuddly and not so popular. In all
these areas, the movement has its heart in the right place.

Its head is another matter. To serious environmentalists,
the owl dispute has become a proxy for the goal of preserving
old-growth forests. In private many enviros acknowledge that
owl extinction claims have been extensively pressurized with
hot air. They justify this on the grounds that a valid goal, old-
growth forest preservation, is served. Indeed, old-growth preservation is important for the protection of biodiversity, for
conservation of what remains of America's pre-European heritage, and against the prospect that ancient forests may someday be understood to play an irreplaceable ecological role of
which men and women are not yet aware. These are ample
reasons why logging in the Pacific Northwest should be closely
regulated.

Yet an argument based on forest preservation for its own
sake would, in the long run, be stronger than specious species

arguments. After all, if conservation rules are based on an owl extinction claim that research someday disproves, why shouldn't hell-bent logging resume? Whether spotted owls are really endangered raises the whole question of whether conservation can be placed on a secure, rational foundation that outlives alarmist fads.

"I know they're here," said Lowell Diller as he and I stood in the gathering dusk in a redwood glade outside the forest town of Eureka, California. We had hiked to a spot where Diller had previously marked a nest. For fifteen minutes he hooted to summon the owl pair that lived there. Though we saw no shadows moving in the near-dark, Diller was convinced that the owls were observing the intrusion . . . .

Suddenly, no more than fifteen feet away, furry outlines resolved into view. Two spotted owl had conducted their flying approach through a dense forest understory without making any sound audible to us. The owls, who doubtless heard our clumsy footsteps a mile off, regarded us, perhaps wondering, How can these bipeds survive when they make so much noise in the forest?

A Profusion of Spotted Owl

The owl extinction alarm is predicated on two notions: that spotted owl live only in ancient forests, and that a last, fragile, dwindling population of the northern spotted exists mainly in Oregon and Washington. New research suggests that neither notion is true. California does not end at the Golden Gate; between there and the Oregon border lies a 300-mile corridor of mostly Sierra Nevada forest. This vast woodland, ignored in the owl debate, may contain a profusion of spotted owl.

Diller is a wildlife biologist employed by the firm Simpson Timber. In 1990 he began to survey a northern California tract of medium-age, "managed" timberland owned by that company. Since then, he has found and banded 603 spotted owls. Federal documents assume that only 653 owl pairs exist in the whole of California, and that essentially none lives in private timberland. Diller's 603 owls were found by inspection of a small snippet of the Sierra Nevada. Most California woodlands have never been surveyed for owls.

The primary federal document on which the Northwest logging ban is based assumes that "somewhere between 3,000 and 4,000" pairs of spotted owls exist in the United States. Last year [1993] Steven Self and Thomas Nelson, researchers employed by Sierra Pacific, a timber company with a progressive reputation, estimated that California alone is home to between 6,000 and 8,000 spotted owl pairs. Of course, the efforts of Diller, Self and Nelson are backed by industry, which has a financial stake in debunking owl alarms. But then, works of owl pessimism, such as the Audubon report, have been backed by advocacy groups with a financial stake in advancing the same alarms.

Federal spotted owl research has concentrated on Oregon and Washington, the states with the mature, monocultural Douglas fir stands traditionally assumed to be the bird's exclusive habitat. Diller is among the first researchers to look for spotted owl in California. "If research had started in California, the spotted owl would not now be considered endangered," he says.

A significant aspect of Diller's work is that he finds spotted owl reproducing in young woodlands managed by foresters, areas environmental doctrine presumes the bird cannot abide. "The northern spotted owl rarely if ever successfully fledges young from any habitat except old-growth," the Audubon Society declared in 1988. One active nest Diller showed me was not only in a tree glade of medium height and age but was within sight of a logging road where trucks rumble past almost daily. Because Diller has turned up so many owls, his work has backfired on his employer. Simpson Timber has had to file plans that place about 50,000 of its acres into pure preservation status and to restrict company logging in other ways, since tree harvests that might "take" a spotted owl are essentially forbidden even on private land. Meanwhile, Diller's findings have inspired others to begin systematic owl surveys of the vast northern California forest. Agencies such as the California Department of Fish and Game have found spotted owl living and reproducing in several types of non-ancient woodlands, including oak savannas—low-tree habitats unlike any in the Cascade Range of Washington and Oregon. . . .

Sustainable Logging

Deforestation commenced in the United States roughly two centuries ago in New England, as timber was cut or woods were burned for cropland. About a century ago destructive logging practices began to end in New England, while cropland began to be returned to forest as the stirrings of high-yield agriculture reduced the acres needed for cultivation. New Hampshire was 50 percent forest in about 1850; it is now 86 percent forest, though its population has expanded sixfold. Massachusetts was 35 percent forest in about 1850 and is now 59 percent forest.

Likewise, the Southeast began to be deforested about a century ago and then to reforest about half a century ago. Today the Southeast has far more forested acres than prewar, despite a population boom. Deforestation peaked in Western Europe prewar [World War II], then was supplanted by aforestation; today the European Union nations have more forest than fifty years ago, though their human population has nearly doubled. Because the Pacific Northwest was the last place in the United States to which determined logging spread, the deforestation trough there was not reached until the 1980s . . . . But in that decade Northwest timber firms began planting far more trees than they cut; the reforestation cycle commenced. So long as future logging is held at sustainable levels, the Northwest forest is likely to exhibit the rapid recovery observed everywhere else in the developed world.

Formal warning of spotted owl extinction was not tendered until the 1986 Audubon report said that the spotted owl population was teetering toward the doomsday number of 1,500 pairs. In the report's wake, the northern spotted was "listed" under the Endangered Species Act. Coincident to the listing, a government science panel headed by biologist Jack Ward Thomas concluded that federal policy should ensure that a minimum of 3,000 owl pairs are protected. In 1991 federal Judge William Dwyer banned most logging in Oregon and Washington to assure survival of 3,000 owl pairs. At this point the notion of owl doomsday locked in legally. It has not been questioned since. . . .

No Support for Environmentalists' Claims

Environmentalists hold that even if many spotted owl thrive in California, logging bans must continue in Washington and Oregon because owl populations there are locally distinct; the birds roost in cool climates feeding on arboreal squirrels, a "distinct" Northwest delicacy. This is probably an accurate reading of the Endangered Species Act as written, but it points to a deep logical fault in environmental orthodoxy. If local variations in climate and diet convert creatures to different species, a black man who lives in Seattle, gets rained on and eats salmon would be a different species from a white man who lives in stifling humidity in Louisiana and dines on gumbo. By this theory the human race contains hundreds of species. The sort of people likely to be environmentalists maintain that when it comes to genus homo [humans], all individuals of all origins are exactly the same in genetic heritage. Yet when it comes to animals, the tiniest distinction renders apparently identical living things irrevocably separate species. The typical northern and California spotted owls look and act more alike than the typical black American and white African. But according to politically correct dogma, different people are identical while similar birds are drastically different. . . .

Could it be that spotted owls are not endangered but other old-growth species are? Perhaps the replacement of many old-growth forests with young timberlands has caused a wipe-out among creatures harder to count than owls. Current environmental thinking holds that deforestation is the worst form of human activity from the standpoint of biodiversity loss. And there is no doubt that until roughly the past decade, Northwest timber companies slicked off the Cascade Range without regard for conservation. Since the 1991 logging suspension, environmentalists' legal maneuvers have concentrated on expanding the ban's scope to protect some 1,400 non-owl species presumed to be imperiled old-growth obligates. Yet . . . only a handful of the presumably imperiled obligates has been shown to exhibit worrisome population trends. And thus far there are no known extinctions of animals or vascular plants in the forest regions of Washington, Oregon or California, according to The Nature Conservancy and the Environmental Defense Fund. A half-dozen plants are "missing in action" (not observed recently, though known to prosper elsewhere) and mammals such as the red vole and fisher are believed to be declining in population—but so far, no known postwar extinctions. This in a habitat range that has not only been subjected to extensive logging but also numbers among the most intensely studied in the world and is therefore a place where extinctions are likely to be detected. Combined with the prospect that there are many more spotted owl pairs than previously estimated, this raises the question of whether the owl doomsday, which has cost thousands of honest people their livelihoods and occupied the attention of presidents, is at heart a false alarm.

Legitimate Reasons to Preserve Forests

In contrast, the need to preserve forests is no false alarm. Broad agreement exists among researchers that old-growth woodlands require respite from the indiscriminate logging of the postwar era. Unregulated logging left Northwest forests "fragmented"—containing lots of trees, but in blocks chopped into checkerboards. An emerging body of science holds that forest fragmentation imperils biodiversity. For instance, studies suggest that moderate numbers of spotted owl in contiguous "clusters" would be more secure than twice as many owls in fragmented forests. This alone is reason for strict regulation of Northwest logging.

But the clear need for strict regulation of forestry should be argued on its own merits, not by resorting to dubious claims of owl peril. . . .

Consider that as U.S. timber production declines, demand for foreign timber escalates. Many countries will import more wood from nations such as Malaysia and Brazil, where forestry may be summarized by the cry "timmm-burrr!" Today, Japanese firms are slicking off the lush Sarawak rain forest in Malaysia to feed a global wood market energized by U.S. logging bans. In the Sarawak there are no niceties about sustainable yield or protection of species, and there are no well-funded litigators to sue the irresponsible. Moving logging from Oregon to Malaysia may shift the problem out of sight and out of mind. But it is not much of a deal for the environment.

Consider that anti-logging sentiment born of the desire to protect old-growth stands requiring centuries to restore now spills over into activism against logging in young forests easily restored. In 1990 a California ballot initiative nearly banned most logging even on tree plantations. Yet when commercial forestry produces ample tree harvests, the pressure to log out ancient forests declines. "High-yield forestry can work in concert with old-growth preservation," says Michael Oppenheimer, chief scientist for the Environmental Defense Fund.

Consider that from 9,500 (the White House's own number) to 85,000 jobs will be abrogated by the Clinton owl plan. The lost jobs are high-wage employment of the sort that Americans who aren't lawyers or consultants need to send their children to college. Lumber prices have also nearly doubled since the 1991 ban was imposed, adding roughly $5,000 to the price of a new home. This increase is regressive, hitting the working class much harder than the elite environmentalist class.

If it is eventually understood that affluent environmentalists with white-collar sinecure destroyed thousands of desirable skilled-labor jobs in order to satisfy an ideology and boost the returns on fund-raising drives, a long-lasting political backlash against environmentalism will set in. There is still time to avoid this turn of events. Ancient forests can be protected, additional timber jobs restored and the constructive political power of environmentalism sustained. Honesty about owls would be the beginning.

"The lesson of the spotted owl could not be more clear: the long-term health of the economy is compatible with . . . the long-term health of our ecology."

Seattle Audubon Shows That a Healthy Economy Can Coexist with a Healthy Environment

Ernie Niemi, Ed Whitelaw, and Elizabeth Grossman

In the following viewpoint Ernie Niemi, Ed Whitelaw, and Elizabeth Grossman maintain that logging bans enacted to protect the spotted owl did not destroy Oregon's economy as predicted but actually fueled an economic boom there. While reduced logging did negatively impact some of Oregon's residents—primarily loggers—the majority of the people there are actually better off today, argue the authors. In their opinion, the spotted owl case proves not only that a healthy economy can coexist with a healthy ecosystem, but that a healthy ecosystem actually seems to contribute to the long-term health of the economy. Niemi is an economist with ECONorthwest, an economic and financial consulting firm in Oregon; Whitelaw is a professor of economics and president of ECONorthwest; and Grossman is a writer who lives in Oregon.

Remember the uproar over the spotted owl? Everyone said the roof would cave in on the Pacific Northwest economy. Here's what really happened.

It was the early 1990s, and there was no issue hotter than the northern spotted owl. "We'll be up to our neck in owls,

Ernie Niemi, Ed Whitelaw, and Elizabeth Grossman, "Bird of Doom . . . or Was It?" *The Amicus Journal*, vol. 22, Fall 2000, p. 19. Copyright © 2000 by the Natural Resources Defense Council. Reproduced by permission of the authors.

and out of Work for every American," said President George Bush. Congressman Bob Smith (R-OR) declared that saving the Spotted owl would "take us to the bottom of a black hole" A headline in *Business Week* screamed, "The Spotted Owl Could Wipe Us Out."

"That little furry-feathery guy," as Bush called the previously obscure bird, lives only in old-growth forests of Washington, Oregon, and northern California. The forests were being logged into oblivion, and environmentalists had seized on the owl as a way to save them. In lawsuit after lawsuit, they argued that cutting in the national forests had to stop, or the owl would become extinct. And as lawsuit after lawsuit hit the media, the spotted owl became the scariest creature in the country, an industrial-grade economic villain.

Dependence on Logging

In those days, too many Northwesterners believed timber drove the region's economy. The prospect of massive logging reductions set off a panic. Politicians, economic forecasters, logging industry executives, and the media fanned the flames. Dire predictions fed on one another: mill towns would become ghost towns. The entire region would be plunged into a deep recession and might never recover.

The American Forest Resources Association, a timber industry group, estimated that protecting the owl would reduce total employment in Oregon alone by 102,000. Pro-industry academics predicted a loss of some 150,000 jobs. University of Washington sociologist Robert Lee warned, "A permanent rural underclass will be created."

It was a classic case of the superstition that you can't have both a healthy environment and a healthy economy. But a funny thing happened on the way to the future: the sky didn't fall. Not only were job losses due to the owl radically less than predicted—orders of magnitude less—but, economically, the

Pacific Northwest has been one of the biggest success stories of a hugely successful decade.

Road to Salvation?

Lost in the uproar was the fact that the owl was never the main point. "The goal of the lawsuits was to protect the ancient forests of the Pacific Northwest," says Todd True, one of the two lawyers who handled the litigation for the Sierra Club Legal Defense Fund (now known as Earthjustice). "Over the course of the 1980s, it became apparent that an entire ecosystem was being liquidated."

In 1988, the group brought the first of several suits to save the coastal old-growth forests. Its first target was the U.S. Fish and Wildlife Service, which had refused to admit that the owl was at risk of extinction. Once the owl made the federal "threatened" list, Earthjustice was able to sue the government agencies that were selling off owl habitat on public land—the last of the biggest, oldest trees—to the timber companies.

The watershed ruling, by U.S. District judge William Dwyer of Seattle, came down in May 1991. It shook the timber industry and stunned politicians, government officials, and the public. Dwyer found that the U.S. Forest Service and other federal agencies had committed "a remarkable series of violations of the environmental laws" by treating the forests as timber reserves rather than ecosystems. Until those violations were reversed, he said, the Service could sell no timber from critical spotted owl habitat.

Dwyer banned logging on some 24 million acres in seventeen national forests. The move, reinforced by other events, virtually shut down the timber program in national forests in the Pacific Northwest. From 1988 to 1997, the amount of federal timber cut in Oregon and Washington fell from 6.4 billion board feet (bbf) to less than 1.0 bbf—a drop of 87 percent. The overall timber take, from federal, state, and private lands, fell by almost half.

The health of the forests and of the spotted owl itself, Todd True points out, is still in doubt. But he adds, without exaggeration, that the lawsuits caused "a sea change."

"A Very Scary Time"

For more than twenty years, Lane County native Terry Barrett worked in timber. The Weyerhaeuser sawmill in Springfield, Oregon, that employed him processed old growth, and the company had been honest about the fact that its long-term prospects were not good. Regardless, when Barrett was finally laid off, it came as a shock. "It was not a good thing." he says, quietly. "My wife was pregnant with our fourth child, and there I was losing my job and benefits and paid vacation. It was a very scary time."

But Barrett had an advantage: he lives in the Eugene-Springfield area of Lane County, which used to call itself the "lumber capital of Oregon" but is now humming with very different kinds of economic activity. The county is on the I-5 corridor that links cities of the Willamette Valley with Seattle, and it has profited from high technology, a diversity of industry, and a network of local colleges and universities. Opportunities like these have allowed some former timber workers, Terry Barrett among them, to have successful second acts.

Barrett was laid off in August 1990, not long before Judge Dwyer's ruling. At the time, he recalls, competition was so stiff for Lane Community College's training programs that there were more than 600 applicants for 17 openings. Yet he managed to persuade an instructor to let him attend a class that was overenrolled. This persistence, as well as his flexibility, has clearly been an asset for Barrett in his life after timber. He studied math and science, with his eye on a nursing degree, but when that program filled up he chose dental hygiene.

Today, at fifty-one, Barrett can boast a strikingly happy recovery from mid-life career derailment. He is a professional dental hygienist. He makes twice as much money at this job as when he was in timber, and likes it better. But the experience of losing a career and having to get back on his feet has left him wary. To give his children the educational advantages starting out that he lacked—his father left school in the seventh grade, his mother in the ninth—Barrett works no fewer than three additional jobs: in a second dental office, delivering newspapers, and as a part-time mechanic. "It's been a difficult time for a lot of people," he says, "but I enjoy the challenge."

Chicken Little Was Wrong

In all likelihood, Terry Barrett's success in building a professional second career is unusual for out-of-work loggers. Nevertheless, his recovery is a microcosm of, and was made possible by, what happened to the Pacific Northwest as a whole. Throughout the past decade, the region has boomed. Whether you look at jobs, income, or sheer economic exuberance, the Pacific Northwest has consistently outperformed the national Economy. . . .

Decline and Fall

Long before most people had even heard of the spotted owl, the timber industry in the Pacific Northwest had been shrinking. Loggers and millworkers had been living with the threat of layoffs for decades. The reason had nothing to do with endangered species. The industry was simply running out of trees.

Logging companies had been cutting old-growth forests at unsustainable rates since at least World War II. It was no secret that, sooner or later, the party would be over. In fact, the real era of job losses in timber, University of Wisconsin analysts have found, was the late 1940s through the early 1960s.

The cost-cutting years of the 1980s saw another heavy round of layoffs. Timber companies were facing increased global competition, and new automated technologies were coming on line—technologies that allowed one millworker to do the work of many. The notorious industry practice of sending raw logs to Japan and elsewhere in Asia, instead of to local mills, also peaked in this period; before 1991 about a quarter of the logs felled in Washington and Oregon were exported. All these factors allowed industry to break the unions and lay off thousands of workers in the eighties. Timber employment and wages in the two states dropped about 20 percent.

By 1988, when the spotted owl lawsuits were just starting, timber jobs accounted for only 3.6 percent of total employment in Oregon and Washington. By 1994, even the number of jobs added each year in all sectors in the two states was more than total timber industry employment. Timber had become marginal. And owl or no owl, there was worse to come.

In reality, it wasn't the spotted owl that shut the timber industry down. The logging companies were already doing an excellent job of that all on their own. Researchers at Oregon State who looked at the state of the forests said as much in the 1970s, and again in 1990. They foresaw a massive drop in logging sometime in the nineties, when the companies would finally eat their way through the last of the old growth. All the spotted owl suits did was hasten the inevitable—and, of course, make sure there were still a few trees left. . . .

Lost Jobs

Just how many workers did lose their jobs because of the spotted owl? There are many holes in the recordkeeping, but what data are available for Oregon and Washington point to a figure between 6,200 and 9,300. Others put the number in the same ballpark. Eban Goodstein of Lewis and Clark College has estimated that between 6,200 and 7,500 jobs had been lost as of 1994. In 1998, a University of Wisconsin study found that, in the context of the other changes taking place in the industry, the spotted owl had no significant effect on timber employment in the region.

71

Federal assistance brought some relief. The Northwest Economic Adjustment Initiative, for instance, distributes up to $12 million a year for retraining. As of 1998, the initiative had helped nearly 16,000 dislocated timber workers.

The U.S. Department of Labor has found that most of those who lost their timber work found new jobs within a year. Whether the new jobs were as good as the old ones is another question. "I'm the only person I know who has a better job and makes more money than I did before," says Terry Barrett. "The bulk of people I know have reentered the workforce in a lower-paying capacity." These were men who had a family, a mortgage, a camper, and a boat, he says: "It's been tough."

But it's worth keeping in mind that, although many families and towns suffered heavily, even the highest estimates of jobs that disappeared after the Dwyer decision are small compared with the total population. In 1991, Oregon and Washington had 7.9 million people, and employment stood at 3.4 million. The 9,300 timber-related jobs, at most, that might have been lost to the spotted owl represent only 0.3 percent of the total. And they are a far cry indeed from the inflammatory predictions that 100,000 to 150,000 people would be put out of work.

Forests and the New Economy

It was an anticlimax almost on a par with the Y2K computer scare.[1] Disaster never arrived. Logging on 24 million acres of federal lands fell by nearly 90 percent, and the economy just kept getting better. The diminished role of timber in the region was a big factor, but there was another reason. A healthy environment, it turns out, is economically valuable.

---

1. Due to a flaw in computer program design, it was widely feared that at 12 A.M. on January 1, 2000, computer errors would cause many critical industries and government functions to stop working. These fears turned out to be vastly exaggerated.

Northern spotted owls reside in the ancient forests of the Pacific Northwest. The Seattle Audubon *decision attempted to balance the economy with a healthy ecosystem.* Photos.com

A decade ago, many people believed that timber, mining, farming, and other extractive industries made up the foundation of any economy. It's still a popular theory, especially

73

where timber, mining, and agribusiness lobbyists are hard at work keeping it alive. But if the old theory ever was true, it's been left in the dust by today's economy.

The Pacific Northwest is a textbook example. The region is experiencing its biggest boom in the service and high-technology sectors. Say "high-tech," and Microsoft leaps to mind, with its 18,000 employees in the Puget Sound area. But the high-tech transformation is taking place in many other sectors throughout the economy—electronics, computer hardware and service, dot-coms, and even junkyards, for instance. In size, the new employers range all the way down to little companies such as Inovec, which manufactures automation equipment for lumber mills and employs a grand total of fifty people. As early as 1993, the high-tech industry in Oregon and Washington had already overtaken the timber industry in payroll size: $1.9 billion to timber's $1.5 billion.

For employers in a booming, increasingly global economy with low unemployment, environment matters. "The quality of life in the Pacific Northwest is unequivocally a recruiting advantage Amazon.com has over our competitors," says Daniel Malarkey, director of business development at Amazon.com in Seattle. "There's something special about the physical grandeur of the place," he adds. "There's no question that the kinds of people Amazon wants to attract—highly educated, motivated people—these are the kinds of people who enjoy the area's natural amenities." In fact, a 1998 survey by the Oregon Employment Department found that nearly half of new residents had moved to the state primarily because of its quality of life.

What this means is something that would have sounded radical back in 1991: the Pacific Northwest has prospered not in spite of but, in part, because of the logging restrictions. Healthy forests do a lot more for the quality of life than stumps. Clean water is more important to economic health than streams muddied by logging roads, scenic vistas are more important than clearcuts, and whole, wild ecosystems are more important than isolated fragments of forest. And the region's single most effective economic development strategist, by a mile, has been Judge William Dwyer.

Fast-Forward

The lesson of the spotted owl could not be more clear: the long-term health of the economy is compatible with—and probably depends on—the long-term health of our ecology.

But there's little evidence yet that politicians, the media, or the public have learned this lesson. Across the country, the "economy vs. environment" myth persists. In Michigan, Minnesota, and the Rockies, wolves are pitted against farmers and ranchers. In Alabama, would-be coastal developers face off against an endangered beach mouse. Farmers who want the middle Rio Grande for irrigation are up in arms against the silvery minnow. Everywhere, the debates are framed as a choice between jobs and endangered species.

The most obvious, and arguably the most odious, example is the controversy over the lower Snake River in eastern Washington State. One of the options proposed for restoring its vanishing populations of wild salmon is the breaching of four dams to restore 140 miles of free-flowing river. A chorus of fisheries biologists has supported the idea. Yet the Clinton administration has tabled it for five or more years, in response, possibly, to an outcry of opposition that sounded like Spotted Owl II. Breaching the dams "would be an unmitigated disaster and an economic nightmare for the region," warned Washington senator Slade Gorton. Said George W. Bush, "breaching the dams would be a big mistake. . . . The economy and jobs of much of the Northwest depend on the dams." [Former vice president] Al Gore spoke of possible "sweeping economic upheaval." The *Oregonian,* Portland's newspaper, compared breaching the dams to "taking a sledgehammer to the Northwest economy."

Upheaval? A sledgehammer? Hardly. Take a look at what the dams actually accomplish. They help just thirteen farming enterprises to irrigate 37,000 acres—less than half of 1 percent of the total irrigated land in Washington, Oregon, and Idaho. They supply about 4 percent of the electric power in a region that has some of the cheapest electricity rates going. Or look at the analysis of the Army Corps of Engineers, which often takes a pro-development perspective. The Corps predicts a net loss of 1,081 long-term jobs if the dams are breached (4,200 jobs gained, 5,281 jobs lost). For Washington, Oregon, and Idaho, this amounts to about one-fiftieth of 1 percent of all jobs this year [2000].

"Facts, as such, never settled anything," said author and businessman Clarence Randall. Maybe not, but when it comes to the environment, Americans don't seem willing even to listen to the facts. How else to explain the Clinton administration's decision to postpone its Snake River proposal for five years—by which time the salmon may be conveniently extinct?[2]

Our politicians, our media, and our perceptions keep returning to the same old battle lines, the same predictions of economic catastrophe, the same rhetoric, and the same simplistic logic of endangered species vs. endangered jobs.

Until we learn to think clearly about our environment, we are going to lose out. Future generations will lose out too. Terry Barrett, who has experienced the facts of the spotted owl case firsthand, knows where he comes down. "I would love to have my grandchildren see trees like I've seen," he says. "When I went to work in the woods when I was fifteen, there were trees 8 to 10 feet across. I think the conservationists are right. We need to save as much as we can."

2. As of this writing, the dams had not been breached.

"Lawsuits raise an issue's visibility . . .
[and help] to win over the uncommitted
public and persuade elected officials that
the issue is salient."

The Rhetorical Battle over Jobs
Versus the Environment

Judith A. Layzer

Public opinion frequently plays an important role in the resolu-
tion of environmental disputes, explains Judith A. Layzer in the
following viewpoint. She believes the case of the northern spotted
owl illustrates this phenomenon. When environmentalists filed
lawsuits to protect the spotted owl and the forests it lives in, the
visibility of the issue was greatly increased, says Layzer, galvaniz-
ing public support for both environmentalists and the logging in-
dustry. In her opinion, the dispute ceased to become a matter of
each side trying to persuade the other of the merits of its case;
instead, it became a battle for the support of the public and
policy makers. It was these people who had a powerful influence
over the outcome of the case, says Layzer. Layzer is an assistant
professor of political science at Middlebury College in Vermont.
Her research focuses on U.S. environmental politics.

In the late 1980s, the federal government became embroiled
in one of the most notorious environmental controversies
in the nation's history. At issue was the government's obligation to protect the northern spotted owl, a creature that makes
its home almost exclusively in the old-growth forests of the
Pacific Northwest. The debate transcended disagreement over

Judith A. Layzer, *The Environmental Case: Translating Values into Policy.* Washington,
DC: CQ Press, 2002. Copyright © 2002 by Congressional Quarterly, Inc., published by
CQ Press, a division of Congressional Quarterly, Inc. All rights reserved. Reproduced
by permission.

the fate of any particular species, however; it was yet another eruption of the long-standing confrontation between fundamentally different philosophies about the relationship between humans and nature. It pitted those determined to preserve the vestiges of the nation's old-growth forest against those who feared losing their way of life and the region's historical economic base. . . .

Changing Ideas in Land Management

Beginning in the 1970s . . . the Forest Service and the BLM [Bureau of Land Management] began incorporating environmental values and environmental science into their decision making. This happened in part because new laws required both agencies to hire more environmental scientists; to collect biological data on species, water quality, and other ecosystem amenities; and to take factors such as fish, wildlife, and watershed health into account in planning. In addition, the agencies' new generation of employees was more diverse and grew up in an era when environmentalism was part of mainstream American culture. The infusion of scientific and environmentally oriented personnel, combined with directives to take factors besides resource extraction into account in decision making, contributed to a gradual shift over the 1980s in these agencies' organizational cultures. Agency employees, particularly scientists, began to make more ecologically sound assumptions when generating information on which decisions are based.

Environmental Litigation

Enhancing the influence of environmentally oriented employees on agency decision making has been the increasing number, growing vigilance, and expanding clout of environmental groups concerned about preserving ecosystems. . . . The spotted owl case shows how environmentalists can challenge the dominance of extractive interests. To succeed, advocates transformed scientific claims about the spotted owl and old-growth forests into political symbols and compelling causal stories. Frustrated with the slow pace of BLM and Forest Service responses to the plight of the spotted owl, environmentalists resorted to a tactic that has become a staple of the environmental movement: litigation.

Lawsuits can slow the pace of decision making and prompt the collection of information. Moreover, judicial involvement changes the dynamics of environmental controversies in part by raising the level of scrutiny to which agency decision making is exposed. During the 1970s, the courts became more activist in reviewing regulations, justifying their behavior on the grounds that congressional delegation of vast authority to agencies made them more susceptible to "capture" by particular interests and that judicial intervention was necessary to ensure fairness. While scholars and judges have debated the merits of reviewing the substance or merely the procedures of agency decision making, both approaches have the same goal: getting agencies to "elaborate the basis for their decisions and to make explicit their value choices in managing risks" [according to David M. O'Brien in his 1987 book *What Process Is Due?*]. That, in turn, has elevated environmentally oriented scientists who can provide solutions to the challenges posed by new statutory requirements.

In addition to forcing agencies to justify their decisions, lawsuits raise an issue's visibility, which generally favors previously excluded groups. Forced into the limelight, economic interests retaliate against environmentalists' advocacy with arguments about the reliance of the region's economy on extractive jobs, the importance of low-cost resources for the nation's well-being, and the tradeoff between economic growth and environmental protection. Organizations generate predictions of the economic impacts of imposing environmental restrictions on resource extraction, forecasts that depended heavily on the assumptions used. And, as previous cases have made clear, neither side in this controversy is persuaded by the other; rather, the purpose of both sides' efforts is to win over the uncommitted public and persuade elected officials that the issue is salient. . . .

The Case

While conflict over the spotted owl raged during a fifteen-year period from the mid-1980s through the 1990s, the issue actually arose a decade earlier when agency scientists first sounded the alarm. In 1968, a twenty-two-year-old Oregon State University student named Eric Forsman and his adviser, Howard Wight, had begun to study the biology and ecology of the owl, and they quickly became concerned about Forest Service harvesting practices. By the early 1970s, Forsman was pestering anyone who might be able to help him protect spotted owl habitat: the Corvallis Oregon City Council; the Audubon Society; the Forest Service; and the BLM. Although federal land management agencies were gradually becoming more receptive to scientists' ecological concerns, their long-standing timber bias circumscribed their willingness to act protectively. Eventually, environmentalists, impatient with the pace of policy change, took the agencies to court to force their hand. . . .

Interest Group Confrontations: Lawsuits and PR Campaigns

[In the late 1980s, environmental activists] began pursuing injunctions against logging on the federal lands inhabited by the owl, claiming that neither the Forest Service nor the BLM had satisfied its obligations under NEPA [National Environmental Policy Act], NFMA [National Forest Management Act], the O&C [Oregon and California] Lands Act, the Migratory Bird and Treaty Act, and other laws. In late 1987, the SCLDF [Sierra Club Legal Defense Fund] represented Portland Audubon and other environmental groups in a lawsuit challenging the

BLM's logging of spotted owl habitat in Oregon (*Portland Audubon Society v. Lujan*). In 1988, a Portland judge, Helen Frye, issued a temporary injunction that halved timber harvesting on BLM lands in Oregon. The Seattle chapter of the National Audubon Society, the Oregon Natural Resources Council (ONRC), and more than a dozen other plaintiffs also filed suit challenging the adequacy of the Forest Service's plans to safeguard the owl (*Seattle Audubon Society v. Robertson*). The plaintiffs convinced Federal District Judge William Dwyer to enjoin the Forest Service from conducting timber sales scheduled for 1989. These temporary injunctions had dramatic effects: they halted 165 timber sales throughout the Pacific Northwest, slashing the amount of timber available for harvesting on federal lands in 1989 from 5.4 billion board feet to 2.4 billion board feet.

Environmentalists recognized that, in the long run, they needed more than legal support for their position, however. Furthermore, they knew the battle could not simply be waged in Oregon and Washington, where timber was a pillar of the economy. Ultimately, they would have to create a vocal, national constituency for the old-growth forest by persuading millions of Americans that, even if they did not live in the Pacific Northwest, they needed to protect the old-growth forest because it was a national treasure. The environmentalists' national PR [public relations] campaign was manifold: they coined the term "ancient forest" to describe the area; sponsored hikes, tours, and flyovers to capitalize on the shocking visual impacts of clearcutting; wrote articles for national magazines from the *New Yorker* to *National Geographic;* and toured the country with a giant redwood in tow to dramatize the plight of the Northwest's trees.

While mainstream environmental groups pursued conventional means, more radical groups engaged in guerrilla tactics. Earth First! members, for instance, camped out on plywood platforms in trees scheduled to be cut down. They sat on boxes of company dynamite to prevent blasting, spiked trees, set their feet in cement-filled ditches, chained themselves to timber equipment, and buried themselves in rocks to stop bulldozers from moving up logging roads. Their approach did not always engender sympathy for their cause, but it made mainstream environmentalists appear reasonable by comparison.

The Timber Industry Response

Although the timber industry would have preferred to resolve the conflict locally, where its influence was greatest, it did not react passively to environmental activism. Timber workers quickly organized themselves into coalitions, such as the 72,000-member Oregon Lands Coalition. Like the environmentalists, these groups recognized the power of rhetoric and display. On July 1, 1989, the First Annual American Loggers Solidarity Rally came to Forks, Washington, the self-proclaimed timber capital of the world. A reporter for *Audubon* magazine describes the scene, as hundreds of logging trucks rolled into town honking their horns:

> Yellow balloons and flags and legends. "No timber, no revenue, no schools, no jobs." Over a picture of a mechanical crane: "These birds need habitats, too." On the side of a truck: "Enough is enough!" In the hands of a child: "Don't take my daddy's job." On a sandwich board: "Our Ancient Trees are Terminally Ill."

Speaker after speaker at the rally derided environmentalists as frivolous and selfish. . . .

Ultimately, big timber, fearing their lands would be scrutinized next, joined the smaller operators in working aggressively behind the scenes to counteract environmentalists' pressure. They made substantial campaign contributions to candidates supporting their position and worked through their lobbying organizations, the American Forest Resource Alliance (AFRA) and the National Forest Products Association

(NFPA), to assemble evidence supporting their argument that the government should not protect the owl until scientists were certain the bird was endangered. To mobilize popular sentiment, industry groups submitted editorials and took out advertisements in local newspapers. Since environmentalists had nationalized the issue, logging supporters also worked to transform the issue into a concern of carpenters, builders, and consumers nationwide. They activated allies in industries that relied on cheap wood, such as the National Homebuilders Association, which ran a full-page ad in newspapers blaming the spotted owl for "soaring lumber prices." . . .

Congress Takes Up the Issue

By 1990, the spotted owl was front-page news across the country, and in the legislative session that followed, some ambitious members of Congress crafted legislation to protect the old-growth forest in hopes of capitalizing on national concern. The House Interior Subcommittee on National Parks and Public Lands and the House Agriculture Subcommittee on Forests, Family Farms, and Energy each debated forest protection bills in 1990. Neither pleased environmentalists, who argued the timber levels were too high, or timber lobbyists, who argued they were too low. . . .

In May 1991, environmentalists won their battle in Judge Dwyer's court to block all new Forest Service timber sales in the old-growth forest until the service could present an acceptable plan to protect the spotted owl habitat. . . .

A Political Battle

The spotted owl challenge was a litmus test for federal land managers trying to adjust to environmentalism. With its spectacular old-growth forests, combined with a historic economic dependence on timber, the region was a powder keg waiting to be ignited, and the spotted owl provided the spark. For over a decade, the Forest Service and BLM, the two agencies

83

primarily responsible for managing the owl's habitat, wrestled quietly with protecting it while maintaining timber harvest levels. Although agency scientists accumulated compelling evidence suggesting that the owl and its dwindling old growth were in trouble, the agencies' long-standing commitments to timber harvesting, as well as political pressure from the region's elected officials, made a dramatic departure from the status quo unlikely. Agency scientists found themselves isolated, as political appointees tried to steer policy in directions decided by political expediency rather than science.

Frustrated with the slow pace of change in agency priorities, environmentalists filed lawsuits in hopes of changing the political dynamics of the issue. Court rulings in Washington and Oregon changed the status quo radically, from extensive logging to no logging of old-growth forests. The litigation elevated ecology and conservation biology relative to timber harvesting and raised the status of agency scientists who had been overruled in the 1970s and early 1980s but now offered the only way through the impasse at which the agencies found themselves. Court-ordered injunctions also helped environmentalists raise the national visibility of preserving old-growth forests, a phenomenon that was manifested in the candidates' attention to the issue during the 1992 presidential campaign, as well as in a burgeoning number of congressional proposals to protect the region's forests.

The Role of Public Support

The national campaign that ensued highlights the political potency of environment versus economy rhetoric. Whenever environmental regulations are proposed, advocates of natural resource development publicize projections of massive job losses and dire economic repercussions, and the spotted owl controversy was no exception. Wielding studies conducted at the region's universities, as well as by government agencies and timber industry interest groups, opponents of spotted owl protection measures crafted a powerful case about the human costs of such interventions. Environmentalists responded with their own studies suggesting that owl protection measures were not the primary culprit behind lumber price increases or job losses in the region's timber industry. Over time, the relationship between environment and economy has proven to be more complex than either side portrayed it.

CHAPTER 3

Balancing Private Property Rights Against Environmental Conservation

Case Overview

Lucas v. South Carolina Coastal Council (1992)

The protection of private property rights has always been an important American value. Like the right to free speech and the freedom of religion, it is protected by the U.S. Constitution. However it has also been traditionally recognized that property owners have a responsibility to respect the rights and interests of others and the community as a whole. *Lucas v. South Carolina Coastal Council* illustrates the difficulty of balancing these two interests. The 1992 case reveals the conflict that arises between constitutional protections of private property and environmental regulations intended to protect the larger community.

In 1986 businessman David Lucas purchased two lots on the Isle of Palms, South Carolina, for $985,000. His intention was to build homes on these lots. Two years after Lucas's purchase, however, the state passed environmental regulations prohibiting construction on the lots in order to prevent erosion and environmental degradation. Lucas claimed that the law was constitutionally equivalent to a formal effort by the government to take over the ownership of his property and that he was therefore entitled to compensation for the lost development value of the land. A trial court agreed, deciding that Lucas should receive $1.2 million in compensation. The South Carolina Coastal Council, the body responsible for enforcing coastal regulations, appealed to the South Carolina Supreme Court, which reversed the decision. The case then went to the U.S. Supreme Court.

The *Lucas* case centered on a constitutional provision called the takings clause. The Fifth Amendment to the U.S. Constitution prohibits government action that results in the "taking" of private property "without just compensation." The extent of this provision has long been debated. It is widely recognized that if the government takes land for some public purpose such as the construction of a school, a road, or a park, it must financially compensate the owner. However, the courts have also recognized that the government has the right to limit property uses, sometimes severely, to prevent harm to the environment and protect the public welfare. Landowners and conservationists continue to disagree over how far environmental regulations can extend without violating the Fifth Amendment.

In 1992 the Supreme Court ruled that compensation is required when legislation deprives an owner of "all economically beneficial or productive use" of his or her property. It found that because environmental regulations had deprived Lucas of all his land's economic value, a taking had occurred and the government was required to compensate him.

Lucas shows how difficult it often is to find an acceptable balance between private property rights and environmental protection. In this case the ruling was a victory for landowners and a setback for environmentalists. By ruling in favor of David Lucas, the Court affirmed private property rights, a founding principle of American society. However by limiting the extent to which private property owners must take responsibility for environmental protection, the Court weakened the idea that all members of society share the task of protecting the environment.

| "A taking of private property under the Fifth and Fourteenth Amendments [requires a] payment of 'just compensation.'"

The Court's Decision: Property Owners Must Be Compensated for Environmental "Takings"

Antonin Scalia

In the following viewpoint, Justice Antonin Scalia delivers the 1992 opinion of the Supreme Court in Lucas v. South Carolina Coastal Council. *Scalia explains that in 1986 David Lucas purchased land in South Carolina on which he intended to build two homes. However, two years later the South Carolina Legislature enacted environmental regulations preventing that construction. According to Scalia, because these regulations deprived Lucas of all economic value to be derived from his land, they constituted an outright taking of his property. Thus, he says, as required by the takings clause of the Fifth Amendment, the government must compensate Lucas for the economic value of his property. Scalia has served as a justice on the U.S. Supreme Court since 1975.*

In 1986, petitioner David H. Lucas paid $975,000 for two residential lots on the Isle of Palms in Charleston County, South Carolina, on which he intended to build single-family homes. In 1988, however, the South Carolina Legislature enacted the Beachfront Management Act, 48-39250 et seq., which had the direct effect of barring petitioner from erecting any permanent habitable structures on his two parcels. A state

Antonin Scalia, majority opinion, *Lucas v. South Carolina Coastal Council,* 505 U.S. 1003, June 29, 1992.

trial court found that this prohibition rendered Lucas' parcels "valueless." This case requires us to decide whether the Act's dramatic effect on the economic value of Lucas' lots accomplished a taking of private property under the Fifth and Fourteenth Amendments requiring the payment of "just compensation."

South Carolina's expressed interest in intensively managing development activities in the so-called "coastal zone" dates from 1977 when, in the aftermath of Congress's passage of the federal Coastal Zone Management Act of 1972, the legislature enacted a Coastal Zone Management Act of its own. In its original form, the South Carolina Act required owners of coastal zone land that qualified as a "critical area" (defined in the legislation to include beaches and immediately adjacent sand dunes), to obtain a permit from the newly created South Carolina Coastal (Council) (respondent here) prior to committing the land to a "use other than the use the critical area was devoted to." . . .

The Case

In the late 1970's, Lucas and others began extensive residential development of the Isle of Palms, a barrier island situated eastward of the city of Charleston. Toward the close of the development cycle for one residential subdivision known as "Beachwood East," Lucas, in 1986, purchased the two lots at issue in this litigation for his own account. No portion of the lots, which were located approximately 300 feet from the beach, qualified as a "critical area" under the 1977 Act; accordingly, at the time Lucas acquired these parcels, he was not legally obliged to obtain a permit from the Council in advance of any development activity. His intention with respect to the lots was to do what the owners of the immediately adjacent parcels had already done: erect single-family residences. He commissioned architectural drawings for this purpose.

The Beachfront Management Act brought Lucas' plans to an abrupt end. Under that 1988 legislation, the Council was directed to establish a "baseline" connecting the landward-most "point[s] of erosion . . . during the past forty years" in the region of the Isle of Palms that includes Lucas' lots. In action not challenged here, the Council fixed this baseline landward of Lucas' parcels. That was significant, for under the Act, construction of occupable improvements was flatly prohibited seaward of a line drawn 20 feet landward of, and parallel to, the baseline. The Act provided no exceptions.

Seeking Just Compensation

Lucas promptly filed suit in the South Carolina Court of Common Pleas, contending that the Beachfront Management Act's construction ban effected a taking of his property without just compensation. Lucas did not take issue with the validity of the Act as a lawful exercise of South Carolina's police power, but contended that the Act's complete extinguishment of his property's value entitled him to compensation regardless of whether the legislature had acted in furtherance of legitimate police power objectives. Following a bench trial, the court agreed. Among its factual determinations was the finding that, at the time Lucas purchased the two lots, both were zoned for single-family residential construction and . . . there were no restrictions imposed upon such use of the property by either the State of South Carolina, the County of Charleston, or the Town of the Isle of Palms. The trial court further found that the Beachfront Management Act decreed a permanent ban on construction insofar as Lucas' lots were concerned, and that this prohibition deprive[d] Lucas of any reasonable economic use of the lots, . . . eliminated the unrestricted right of use, and render[ed] them valueless. The court thus concluded that Lucas' properties had been "taken" by operation of the Act, and it ordered respondent to pay "just compensation" in the amount of $1,232,387.50.

The Supreme Court of South Carolina reversed.... The court ruled that, when a regulation respecting the use of property is designed "to prevent serious public harm," no compensation is owing under the Takings Clause regardless of the regulation's effect on the property's value....

The Takings Clause

Prior to Justice [Oliver Wendell] Holmes' exposition in *Pennsylvania Coal Co. v. Mahon* (1922), it was generally thought that the Takings Clause reached only a "direct appropriation" of property.... Justice Holmes recognized in *Mahon,* however, that, if the protection against physical appropriations of private property was to be meaningfully enforced, the government's power to redefine the range of interests included in the ownership of property was necessarily constrained by constitutional limits. If, instead, the uses of private property were subject to unbridled, uncompensated qualification under the police power, the natural tendency of human nature [would be] to extend the qualification more and more until at last private property disappear[ed]. These considerations gave birth in that case to the oft-cited maxim that, "while property may be regulated to a certain extent, if regulation goes too far, it will be recognized as a taking."

Nevertheless, our decision in *Mahon* offered little insight into when, and under what circumstances, a given regulation would be seen as going "too far" for purposes of the Fifth Amendment. In 70-odd years of succeeding "regulatory takings" jurisprudence, we have generally eschewed any "'set formula'" for determining how far is too far, preferring to "engag[e] in ... essentially ad hoc, factual inquiries [*Goldblatt v. Hempstead* as quoted in *Penn Central Transportation Co. v. New York City*]." We have, however, described at least two discrete categories of regulatory action as compensable .... The first encompasses regulations that compel the property owner to suffer a physical "invasion" of his property.

In general (at least with regard to permanent invasions), no matter how minute the intrusion, and no matter how weighty the public purpose behind it, we have required compensation. . . .

The second situation in which we have found categorical treatment appropriate is where regulation denies all economically beneficial or productive use of land. As we have said on numerous occasions, the Fifth Amendment is violated when land use regulation "does not substantially advance legitimate state interests or denies an owner economically viable use of his land [*Agins v. City of Tiburon*]."

Total Deprivation of Beneficial Use

We have never set forth the justification for this rule. Perhaps it is simply, as Justice [William] Brennan suggested, that total deprivation of beneficial use is, from the landowner's point of view, the equivalent of a physical appropriation. . . . The functional basis for permitting the government, by regulation, to affect property values without compensation—that Government hardly could go on if, to some extent, values incident to property could not be diminished without paying for every such change in the general law—does not apply to the relatively rare situations where the government has deprived a landowner of all economically beneficial uses. . . .

We think, in short, that there are good reasons for our frequently expressed belief that, when the owner of real property has been called upon to sacrifice all economically beneficial uses in the name of the common good, that is, to leave his property economically idle, he has suffered a taking. . . .

It is correct that many of our prior opinions have suggested that "harmful or noxious uses" of property may be proscribed by government regulation without the requirement of compensation. For a number of reasons, however, we think the South Carolina Supreme Court was too quick to conclude that that principle decides the present case. . . .

Exceptions to Compensation

Where the State seeks to sustain regulation that deprives land of all economically beneficial use, we think it may resist compensation only if the logically antecedent inquiry into the nature of the owner's estate shows that the proscribed use interests were not part of his title to begin with. This accords, we think, with our "takings" jurisprudence, which has traditionally been guided by the understandings of our citizens regarding the content of, and the State's power over, the "bundle of rights" that they acquire when they obtain title to property. It seems to us that the property owner necessarily expects the uses of his property to be restricted, from time to time, by various measures newly enacted by the State in legitimate exercise of its police powers; "[a]s long recognized, some values are enjoyed under an implied limitation, and must yield to the police power." [*Pennsylvania Coal Co. v. Mahon*]. And in the case of personal property, by reason of the State's traditionally high degree of control over commercial dealings, he ought to be aware of the possibility that new regulation might even render his property economically worthless (at least if the property's only economically productive use is sale or manufacture for sale). In the case of land, however, we think the notion pressed by the Council that title is somehow held subject to the "implied limitation" that the State may subsequently eliminate all economically valuable use is inconsistent with the historical compact recorded in the Takings Clause that has become part of our constitutional culture. . . .

We emphasize that, to win its case, South Carolina must do more than proffer the legislature's declaration that the uses Lucas desires are inconsistent with the public interest. . . . Instead, as it would be required to do if it sought to restrain Lucas in a common law action for public nuisance, South Carolina must identify background principles of nuisance and property law that prohibit the uses he now intends in the circumstances in which the property is presently found. Only on this showing can the State fairly claim that, in proscribing all such beneficial uses, the Beachfront Management Act is taking nothing.

> *"This Court repeatedly has recognized the ability of government . . . to regulate property without compensation, no matter how adverse the financial effect on the owner may be."*

Dissenting Opinion: Compensation Is Not Required for Restricted Land Use

Harry A. Blackmun

The following viewpoint is excerpted from Justice Harry A. Blackmun's dissent in Lucas v. South Carolina Coastal Council. *Blackmun maintains that David Lucas, who purchased coastal land in South Carolina in 1986, is not entitled to government compensation for 1988 environmental regulations that prohibit him from building on these lots. As Lucas himself recognizes, building on the land will cause significant coastal erosion, says Blackmun, and a ban on building is thus necessary for the public good. The government has the right to prohibit an owner's use of a property if it will be harmful to the public good and is not required to economically compensate the owner in such cases. Blackmun served on the U.S. Supreme Court from 1970 to 1994. He died in 1999.*

In 1972, Congress passed the Coastal Zone Management Act. The Act was designed to provide States with money and incentives to carry out Congress' goal of protecting the public from shoreline erosion and coastal hazards. In the 1980

Harry A. Blackmun, dissenting opinion, *Lucas v. South Carolina Coastal Council,* 505 U.S. 1003, June 29, 1992.

amendments to the Act, Congress directed States to enhance their coastal programs by "[p]reventing or significantly reducing threats to life and the destruction of property by eliminating development and redevelopment in high-hazard areas."

Efforts to Stop Erosion

South Carolina began implementing the congressional directive by enacting the South Carolina Coastal Zone Management Act of 1977. Under the 1977 Act, any construction activity in what was designated the "critical area" required a permit from the South Carolina Coastal Council; and the construction of any habitable structure was prohibited. The 1977 critical area was relatively narrow.

This effort did not stop the loss of shoreline. In October, 1986, the Council appointed a "Blue Ribbon Committee on Beachfront Management" to investigate beach erosion and propose possible solutions. In March, 1987, the Committee found that South Carolina's beaches were "critically eroding," and proposed land use restrictions. In response, South Carolina enacted the Beachfront Management Act on July 1, 1988. The 1988 Act did not change the uses permitted within the designated critical areas. Rather, it enlarged those areas . . . .

Petitioner [David H.] Lucas is a contractor, manager, and part owner of the Wild Dune development on the Isle of Palms [in South Carolina]. He has lived there since 1978. In December, 1986, he purchased two of the last four pieces of vacant property in the development. The area is notoriously unstable. In roughly half of the last 40 years, all or part of [RA1] petitioner's property was part of the beach or flooded twice daily by the ebb and flow of the tide. Between 1957 and 1963, petitioner's property was under water. Between 1963 and 1973, the shoreline was 100 to 150 feet onto petitioner's property. In 1973, the first line of stable vegetation was about half-way through the property. Between 1981 and 1983, the

Isle of Palms issued 12 emergency orders for sandbagging to protect property in the Wild Dune development. . . .

Protecting the Public Good

The Beachfront Management Act includes a finding by the South Carolina General Assembly that the beach/dune system serves the purpose of "protect[ing] life and property by serving as a storm barrier which dissipates wave energy and contributes to shoreline stability in an economical and effective manner." The General Assembly also found that "development unwisely has been sited too close to the [beach/dune] system. This type of development has jeopardized the stability of the beach/dune system, accelerated erosion, and endangered adjacent property." . . .

Long ago it was recognized that all property in this country is held under the implied obligation that the owner's use of it shall not be injurious to the community, and the Takings Clause [of the Fifth Amendment] did not transform that principle to one that requires compensation whenever the State asserts its power to enforce it. The Court consistently has upheld regulations imposed to arrest a significant threat to the common welfare, whatever their economic effect on the owner.

Petitioner never challenged the legislature's findings that a building ban was necessary to protect property and life. Nor did he contend that the threatened harm was not sufficiently serious to make building a house in a particular location a "harmful" use, that the legislature had not made sufficient findings, or that the legislature was motivated by anything other than a desire to minimize damage to coastal areas. Indeed, petitioner objected at trial that evidence as to the purposes of the setback requirement was irrelevant. The South Carolina Supreme Court accordingly understood petitioner not to contest the State's position that "discouraging new construction in close proximity to the beach/dune area is necessary to prevent a great public harm," and "to prevent serious injury to the community." . . .

Power of the Government to Regulate Property Without Compensation

This Court repeatedly has recognized the ability of government, in certain circumstances, to regulate property without compensation, no matter how adverse the financial effect on the owner may be. More than a century ago [in *Mugler v. Kansas*], the Court explicitly upheld the right of States to prohibit uses of property injurious to public health, safety, or welfare without paying compensation: "A prohibition simply upon the use of property for purposes that are declared, by valid legislation, to be injurious to the health, morals, or safety of the community, cannot, in any just sense, be deemed a taking or an appropriation of property." . . .

More recently, in *Goldblatt [v. Hempstead]* (1902), the Court upheld a town regulation that barred continued operation of an existing sand and gravel operation in order to protect public safety. . . .

These cases rest on the principle that the State has full power to prohibit an owner's use of property if it is harmful to the public. "[S]ince no individual has a right to use his property so as to create a nuisance or otherwise harm others, the State has not 'taken' anything when it asserts its power to enjoin the nuisance-like activity [*Bituminous Coal Assn v. De-Benedictis*]." It would make no sense under this theory to suggest that an owner has a constitutionally protected right to harm others, if only he makes the proper showing of economic loss.

"All law, including environmental regulations, must be based solely on our individual rights to own and use private property."

Environmental Regulations Violate the Rights of Property Owners

Zak Klemmer and Jo Anne Klemmer

In 1992 the U.S. Supreme Court ruled that the government was required to compensate property owner David Lucas for environmental regulations that denied him all economically viable use of his land. In the following viewpoint Zak Klemmer and Jo Anne Klemmer agree with the Court's decision but insist there should be no environmental regulations on private property owners in the first place. Such regulations violate people's individual rights to own and use private property, argue the authors, subordinating Americans' freedom to the power of the government. In addition, they maintain, land-use restrictions weaken the economy by unnecessarily obstructing commercial development. At the time of the original publication, Zak Klemmer was a designer with M3 Engineering and Technology in Tucson, Arizona. Jo Anne Klemmer was the business manager of the Tucson Osteopathic Medical Foundation.

When does uncompensated regulation become theft? Environmental regulations have become some of the most obtrusive laws invading private property rights today. Regula-

Zak Klemmer and Jo Anne Klemmer, "Denial of Rights Through Regulation," *The Freeman*, vol. 43, June 1993. Copyright © 1993 by Foundation for Economic Education, Inc., www.fee.org. All rights reserved. Reproduced by permission.

tory taking gave rise to *Lucas v. South Carolina Coastal Commission*, decided last year [1992] by the U.S. Supreme Court.

The *Lucas* Case

David Lucas paid $975,000 in 1986 for two beach-front lots on which he planned to build two houses, one for himself and one to sell. A state agency barred the construction under an environmental law that took effect two years after he purchased the lots. Lucas sued the state of South Carolina, arguing that the regulation denied him all economically viable use of his land. (It should be pointed out that similar single family houses are adjacent to both sides of Lucas' property.)

The state court agreed with Mr. Lucas' argument and awarded him $1.2 million for the regulatory taking of his property. However, the South Carolina Supreme Court reversed the lower court's decision on appeal, ruling that "a restriction 'enacted to prevent serious public harm' doesn't require a state to compensate landowners for their losses."

This case made its way to the U.S. Supreme Court. In June 1992, Lucas received a six to two vote in his favor. In an opinion for the majority, Justice Antonin Scalia wrote, "Even if a regulation addresses a serious harm, the government must compensate a property owner denied all economically viable use of his land."

Although the decision was favorable for Lucas, it appears that the U.S. Supreme Court's decision was narrowly drawn and did not adequately protect property rights destroyed by land use restrictions. "This was a golden opportunity to 'straighten out' the law on the government taking of property. . . . The court 'blew' the opportunity. . . . It's impossible to tell what it does to a whole range of cases because its effect may be extremely limited," writes Roger Pilon of the Cato Institute.

What land use restrictions achieve is a weakening of our economy by obstructing commercial development. This is a direct and intended result of environmental activism. An overly broad environmental agenda, enforced by expansive regulations with a sluggish legal system, can be as destructive to our economy as confiscatory taxation. The net effect of a regulatory taking of property, as illustrated by *Lucas*, is similar to that of a direct tax, in that it hinders (or in some cases prevents) the property owner's use of his livelihood, his rights.

Nell Simon's Case

Some twenty-five hundred miles away from David Lucas, Nell Simon of Tucson, Arizona, represents the Venture West Group (VWG). This is an investment group founded in Tucson in 1981. The VWG has successfully developed commercial real estate in Phoenix, Denver, and California, as well as Tucson.

Simon, like Lucas, is embroiled in a property regulatory nightmare with environmental do-goodism at its core.

The property in consideration is a 7.1 acre site at Broadway and Houghton, on Tucson's east side. This parcel has been zoned for shopping center use for the entire eleven years that VWG has owned it. Running through the middle of this parcel is a dry wash (approximately 3.2 acres), which traverses into an existing culvert under Broadway Boulevard. Many washes have been culverted along Broadway to accommodate commercial projects.

As a pretext to save the remaining "prime riparian habitat areas" within the city limits of Tucson, no-growth activists lobbied the City Council to pass the Environment Resource Zone Ordinance (ERZ) in 1990. The ERZ Ordinance was intended to prevent the development of 53 miles of designated washes. The parcel at Broadway and Houghton fell under the ERZ. Because its 600-foot-long wash bisects it into two less valuable parcels, Simon sought a variance to allow development of the shopping center. This process began in January 1991.

By December 1991 the City Board of Adjustments unanimously approved the variance. This lengthy process included, among other things, public hearings. The variance, however, was subject to design considerations intended to mitigate the impact of development on the wildlife habitat in the ERZ. These considerations attached additional costs to the project outside the control of the developers and their architects surpassing $100,000. In February 1992 the City Council of Tucson took up the issue and overturned the variance that had been granted by the City Board of Adjustments.

"We want to build the shopping center. We don't want to file a lawsuit," said Simon in reply to the Council's reversal. "The Council's action amounts to an illegal 'taking' of property," declared Sy Short, Simon's attorney. The VWG has filed a lawsuit of $2.5 million against the city for the refusal to allow this proposed shopping center to be built over a culverted wash.

It seems as though government agencies have an endless supply of time and money to obstruct citizens who expect these agencies to respect and honor their constitutional right to own and use private property. One may ask: When does regulation become an obstacle to productivity and progress? And, what occurs when a regulation becomes an end in itself instead of the means to an end? When regulation becomes an end in itself, it perverts the law and usurps the economic freedom it is designed to protect, resulting in poverty and decline. The endless delays and regulations which have been imposed on Simon's project have not only been financially prohibitive, but have detrimentally affected the economic health of the local community by the loss of potential employment.

More Regulation Means a Loss of Jobs

Moving westward to California we locate still more examples of undue regulations brought on by environmental activism. The Council on California Competitiveness (CCC) reported in April 1992 that the growing regulatory burden has become a major hurdle to the state's economic recovery. Since 1990,

700,000 jobs have been lost in California; yet regulatory costs to employers persist. The once proud "Golden State" no longer creates jobs and wealth. It is creating burdensome regulations, exorbitant state government employment, and deficits at record levels. According to the CCC, chaired by Peter Ueberroth, "Laws that were originally passed to protect our quality of life now are being used to thwart environmentally sound economic growth without balancing job impact with economic needs."

Ball Glass Packaging Corporation has been producing glass jars in Santa Ana, California, for the past 60 years and has employed over 300 people. Ball Corporation is closing its doors. Why?

David Westmoreland, vice-president of Ball Corporation stated, "One of the problems we have in the South Coast Air Quality Management District (AQMD) is that we're always chasing a moving target." To be more specific, Westmoreland lamented, "[The Santa Ana plant] has a furnace which is the heart of the operation which by necessity of normal [economic] life will require major repairs next year. But, before that furnace can go through its next life cycle, new rules are passed that make it no longer in compliance. . . . You could put millions into a rebuild only to find out you've been regulated out of business."

An Unreasonable Regulatory Process

Besides the dilemma of financial feasibility, another problem with compliance is dealing with the regulatory agencies. Meeting with enforcers who possess overlapping authority becomes time consuming and frustrating. "These agencies are really not interested in hearing about your troubles. . . . And we've had people say, 'If you can't meet the rules, shut up and get out of here.' Just like that, 'if you can't meet the damned rules, close down. We don't care!'" charged Francis Paladino, senior vice president of operations for the Ball Corporation. Consequently, Ball Corporation will do just that—close down. Those companies who looked to Ball Corporation for their jars will now have to look elsewhere.and, again in California: At a time when South Central Los Angeles desperately needs jobs, one furniture manufacturer (who requests anonymity) said he had to move 500 jobs from Southern California to Mexico because of AQMD regulations governing wood paint. "The primary reason for the move," he said, "was that the air quality rules were neither legitimate nor reasonable. We proved that what they were asking us to do was physically impossible and we demonstrated it, so they gave us a three-month variance."

"Why they thought we could comply in three months, I cannot say," he added. The furniture is still sold in Los Angeles so the manufacturer must now ship materials to Mexico and the finished product from Mexico. This obviously adds to the traffic congestion, tailpipe emissions, and equipment costs of this manufacturer. "We have now doubled our fleet of trucks so the amount of stuff we're putting into the air with [the added] trucks is probably more than we were putting into the air as manufacturers," he said.

A 1990 Department of Commerce survey of manufacturers found that 62 percent of those surveyed cited "streamlining environmental regulations" as an imperative policy goal. In Southern California alone there are 39 agencies with water quality authority, 38 with hazardous waste authority, 17 with air quality authority, and 14 with solid waste authority. Due to this glut of regulatory agencies, Southern California is losing state revenue and employment for its residents with the exodus of businesses. States like Colorado and Nevada have recruited businesses from California by streamlining the regulatory process.

A Needless Financial Burden

The regulatory taking of property implemented by the bureaucracy plunders the rights of property owners and produces a needless financial burden. The hidden cost of complying with these laws is measured by time lost in negotiating the nearly endless maze of local, state, and federal agencies in the permit process, through applying for variances and design changes, defending nuisance suits, and enduring delays in the legal process. All of this dramatically impedes economic growth for each of us by raising the cost of housing and manufactured products, thwarting production of new products, and eliminating employment opportunities.

All law, including environmental regulations, must be based solely on our individual rights to own and use private property. The greatest danger exists in subordinating our rights to the technocracy of the central planners. Communism may be dead or fading in Eastern Europe, but collectivism as a political philosophy is still alive and dangerous to everyone in the industrialized West.

| *"[Decisions such as* Lucas*] limit govern-*
ment's ability to protect the environment
. . . by making it too costly."

Lucas and Similar Cases Weaken Environmental Protection

Forward

Forward *is a biweekly newspaper published in New York City*
that strives to defend democracy and Jewish rights. In the follow-
ing viewpoint Forward *argues that the Supreme Court's deci-*
sions in Lucas v. South Carolina Coastal Council *and in* Palazzolo v. Rhode Island—*a later case that expanded on the*
precedent set by Lucas—*are detrimental to the government's*
power to protect the environment. Due to the Takings Clause of
the Fifth Amendment, upon which these cases are based, the
government cannot seize property without paying for it. How-
ever, cases such as Lucas *require the government to also pay*
compensation for property that merely loses its value due to en-
vironmental regulation, say the editors of Forward. *They argue*
that this situation lessens the power of the government to protect
the environment by making environmental regulations of private
property extremely costly.

Few recent Supreme Court decisions hold more potentially
historic importance than a ruling handed down last week
[June 28, 2001] in an obscure Rhode Island land-use case.

In a 5-4 decision in the case, *Palazzolo v. Rhode Island,* the
court's conservative majority took a major step toward institu-

Forward, "Zealotry on the High Court," vol. cv, July 6, 2001, p. 8. Copyright © 2001
by Forward Newspaper, LLC. Reproduced by permission.

tionalizing an eccentric legal doctrine that aims to limit government's ability to protect the environment and other interests by reinterpreting constitutional guarantees of private property.

Anthony Palazzolo

The case involved a would-be real estate developer, Anthony Palazzolo, who sought to circumvent environmental regulations protecting the state's sensitive coastal wetlands from overdevelopment. Mr. Palazzolo had acquired an 18-acre bit of coastline where he hoped to build private homes or a beach club. His plans were frustrated by state rules protecting the coastal marshes and a freshwater lake nearby. After years of fruitlessly applying for building permits, he sued, claiming the environmental rules deprived him of some $3 million in profits he hoped to realize from the property. After a series of lower courts dismissals, the Supreme Court's conservatives . . . voted (with the liberal Justice John Paul Stevens concurring in one technical aspect) to uphold his right to sue.

The Takings Clause

At the heart of the case is a radical rereading of the Fifth Amendment. Best known for its barrier against self-incrimination, the amendment also specifies: "nor shall private property be taken for public use without just compensation." For two centuries the so-called Takings Clause has been understood to mean just what it says: that government can't seize property without paying for it. Over the last two decades, however, conservative activists have argued that the clause should require compensation even when a property, though not seized, loses potential value as a result of government regulations.

The so-called "regulatory takings" doctrine, brainchild of the conservative Chicago law professor Richard Epstein, was taken up by Reagan-era Justice Department lawyers. It's since spawned a grass-roots movement of right-wing zealots whose unabashed goal is to limit government's ability to protect the environment, labor and other causes by making it too costly.

Their signal legal victory to date was a partial one in the 1992 Supreme Court decision, *Lucas v. South Carolina Coastal Council.* In it the court upheld a right of compensation under the Takings Clause, but only in cases where regulations had eliminated the property's value entirely. Palazzolo takes the principle one giant step further, affirming the property owner's right to sue in a case where the property hasn't lost all its value. The ruling is being hailed as a breakthrough by Takings zealots, led by the Pacific Legal Foundation, which represented Mr. Palazzolo before the high court. Environmentalists and others predict the ruling will unleash a flood of new lawsuits.

> "If government had to compensate people for regulations that reduce the value of their property, more intelligent decisions would be made."

Lucas Shows the Costs of Conservation

Walter Williams

While it is desirable to preserve America's natural habitat and the species that live in it, argues writer Walter Williams in the following viewpoint, environmental policies cannot be based on conservation alone. In Williams's opinion, when creating environmental regulations that affect private property owners, the government must also consider the possible harms of the regulations on these owners. He argues that in some cases these harms outweigh the environmental benefits. Williams cites the case of David Lucas, in which he says the government ignored economic realities and illogically enforced environmental regulations. He suggests that if the government were affected by these regulations instead of the property owners, it might make more intelligent decisions about conservation strategies.

Disagreement with the world's environmentalist wackos doesn't mean that one is for dirty air and water, against conservation and for species extinction. Dr. Richard Stroup, Montana State University professor of economics and senior associate of the Center for Free Market Environmentalism, explains common-sense approaches to environmental issues in his new book, *Economics: What Everyone Should Know About Economics and the Environment.*

Walter Williams, "When It Comes to Land Use, 'Eco-nomics' Rules," *Deseret News,* June 18, 2003, A10. Copyright © 2003 by Deseret News Publishing Company. Reproduced by permission of Walter Williams and Creators Syndicate, Inc.

The Victim of Environmental Regulation

Stroup starts out with the first lesson of economics: There's scarcity. That means more of one thing means less of another.

California's San Bernardino County was just about ready to build a new hospital. That was until the U.S. Fish and Wildlife Department discovered that the endangered flower-loving Delhi Sands fly was found on the site. The county had to spend $4.5 million to move the hospital 250 feet; it also had to divert funds from its medical mission to pay for mandated Delhi Sands fly studies.

Question: Was it worth it? On the benefit side, we have the survival of some Delhi Sands flies, but what about the cost side? How much pain and suffering and perhaps loss of human life was there because millions of dollars were diverted from the hospital's medical mission?

Stroup's analysis warns us that we must always attend to a regulation's unanticipated side-effects. In other words, beneficiaries of a regulation tend always to be easily detected, but the victims are invisible.

Incentives Matter

David Lucas owned shoreline property that the South Carolina government told him he couldn't develop, even though his next-door neighbors developed their property. South Carolina's regulation made his shoreline property virtually worthless. Lucas sued, and the U.S. Supreme Court forced the South Carolina government to pay him $1 million. Once the state was forced to pay Lucas $1 million, it changed its mind about the worth of keeping the shoreline undeveloped. In fact, it sold it to a developer.

South Carolina's actions demonstrate that incentives matter. Costs borne by others will have less of an effect on our choices than when we bear them directly. Environmentalists love it when the government can force private citizens to bear the burden of their agenda, as opposed to requiring that gov-

Protecting the endangered Delhi Sands fly when it was discovered at a building site in California cost the county millions of dollars in revised plans and studies. U.S. Fish and Wildlife Service/Marjory Nelson

ernment pay landowners for property losses due to one regulation or another. It's cheaper, and that means government officials will more readily cave in to environmentalists' demands.

In other words, regulations that stop a landowner from using his land because of the red-cockaded woodpecker, or prevent a farmer from tilling his land because of an endangered mouse, or prevent a homeowner from building a firebreak to protect his home, produce costs that are privately borne. If government had to compensate people for regulations that reduce the value of their property, more intelligent decisions would be made. Besides, if a particular measure will benefit the public, why should its cost be borne privately?

Making Practical Decisions

Environmentalists go berserk whenever there's talk of drilling for the tens of billions of dollars' worth of oil in Alaska's National Wildlife Refuge. Why? It doesn't cost them anything.

Here's what I predict. If we gave environmentalists Alaska's National Wildlife Refuge, you can bet your last dollar that there'd be oil drilling. Why? It would now cost them something to keep the oil in the ground. The Audubon Society owns the Rainey Preserve in Louisiana, a wildlife refuge. There's oil and natural gas on its property, and it has allowed drilling for over half a century. Not allowing drilling, in the name of saving the environment, would have cost it millions of dollars in revenue.

CHAPTER 4

Preserving Endangered Species

Case Overview

Babbitt v. Sweet Home Chapter of Communities for a Great Oregon (1995)

Scientists estimate that thousands of plant and animal species become extinct every year, largely due to human activity. It is widely believed that this loss of biodiversity poses a serious threat to the environment, and many countries have taken various actions to preserve species. In the United States the Endangered Species Act (ESA), passed in 1973, is the most important piece of legislation aiming to preserve endangered species and the ecosystems on which they depend. Upon signing the act, President Richard Nixon explained its rationale when he said, "Nothing is more priceless and more worthy of preservation than the rich array of animal life with which our country has been blessed."

Under the ESA, property owners are required to protect endangered species residing on their property. However, many people insist that the preservation of America's species and ecosystems is primarily the responsibility of the federal government, not private landowners. As a result numerous landowners have filed lawsuits insisting that under the ESA they are not responsible for helping to preserve biodiversity. *Babbitt v. Sweet Home Chapter of Communities for a Great Oregon* (1995) dispelled these challenges, however, establishing that private property owners do have a responsibility to maintain America's biodiversity. The *Sweet Home* decision affirmed the government's right to require private property owners to protect both endangered species and their ecosystems, even if it is financially costly.

Under the ESA, millions of acres of forests, beaches, and wetlands have been protected from degradation and development by the federal government. However, not all endangered species reside on government-owned land. According to a study by the Association of Biodiversity Information and the Nature Conservancy, half of endangered species have at least 80 percent of their habitat on private lands, meaning that the protection of these species must involve individual landowners. The extent to which the government can force these landowners to protect endangered species has become a highly controversial aspect of the ESA, as illustrated by *Sweet Home.*

The 1995 case began when the Sweet Home Chapter of Communities for a Great Oregon—a pro-logging group—challenged the ESA in court, claiming that while the Act prohibited private landowners from hunting and killing endangered species, it was unfair to also expect them to preserve the habitats of these species. The Sweet Home Chapter argued that when Congress passed the ESA, it did not intend private landowners to bear the financial burden of habitat preservation. While a circuit court ruled in favor of Sweet Home, the outcome was appealed and the case passed to the Supreme Court.

The Supreme Court case centered on Section 9 of the ESA, which makes it unlawful for anyone to "take" an animal that has been listed as endangered or threatened. The act defines *take* as "to harass, harm, pursue, . . . wound, [or] kill." In 1975 Secretary of the Interior Bruce Babbitt—one of the people responsible for enforcing the act—defined *harm* to include "significant habitat modification or degradation where it actually kills or injures wildlife." The Sweet Home Chapter contended that this definition was not what the creators of the act intended, maintaining that habitat preservation must be the responsibility of federal agencies because only they have the financial resources to accomplish this task.

In 1995 the Supreme Court upheld Babbitt's definition of *harm,* ruling that private landowners are prohibited from modifying the habitat of endangered species on their property if this will result in the death or injury of these species. The decision was significant because the Court recognized that environmental protection is not just the realm of the government. Instead, it found that even if it is financially costly, private landowners share the responsibility of preserving biodiversity. The ESA continues to be challenged in court today; however, the *Sweet Home* decision remains important because it allows the government to compel landowners to protect the habitats of endangered species, making the ESA a more effective tool for the preservation of biodiversity in America.

> "[The Endangered Species] Act makes it
> unlawful for any person to . . . [cause]
> 'significant habitat modification or deg-
> radation where it actually kills or injures
> wildlife.'"

The Court's Decision: Landowners Cannot Modify the Habitat of Endangered Species

John Paul Stevens

The following viewpoint is excerpted from the U.S. Supreme Court's June 29, 1995, ruling in Babbitt v. Sweet Home Chapter of Communities for a Great Oregon. *Justice John Paul Stevens delivers the majority opinion of the Court regarding the scope of the Endangered Species Act (ESA). He explains that the act was created in order to protect endangered or threatened species from extinction. Therefore, says Stevens, it is illegal not only to directly kill such species but also to cause death indirectly through habitat modification, even if that habitat is privately owned. He argues that this interpretation of the act is reasonable because it is based on a logical definition of the word* harm *and on the intent of Congress in creating the ESA. Stevens has served as a justice on the U.S. Supreme Court since 1975.*

The Endangered Species Act of 1973, (ESA or Act), contains a variety of protections designed to save from extinction species that the Secretary of the Interior designates as

John Paul Stevens, majority opinion, *Babbitt v. Sweet Home Chapter of Communities for a Great Oregon,* 515 U.S. 687, June 29, 1995.

endangered or threatened. Section 9 of the Act makes it unlawful for any person to "take" any endangered or threatened species. The Secretary has promulgated a regulation that defines the statute's prohibition on takings to include "significant habitat modification or degradation where it actually kills or injures wildlife." This case presents the question whether the Secretary exceeded his authority under the Act by promulgating that regulation.

Habitat Modification as Harm

Section 9(a)(1) of the Endangered Species Act provides the following protection for endangered species:

"... With respect to any endangered species of fish or wildlife listed pursuant to section 1533 of this title it is unlawful for any person subject to the jurisdiction of the United States to ... take any such species within the United States or the territorial sea of the United States[.]"

Section 3(19) of the Act defines the statutory term "take":

"The term 'take' means to harass, harm, pursue, hunt, shoot, wound, kill, trap, capture, or collect, or to attempt to engage in any such conduct."

The Act does not further define the terms it uses to define "take." The Interior Department regulations that implement the statute, however, define the statutory term "harm":

"Harm in the definition of 'take' in the Act means an act which actually kills or injures wildlife. Such act may include significant habitat modification or degradation where it actually kills or injures wildlife by significantly impairing essential behavioral patterns, including breeding, feeding, or sheltering."

This regulation has been in place since 1975.

A limitation on the [Section] 9 "take" prohibition appears in 10(a)(1)(B) of the Act, which Congress added by amendment in 1982. That section authorizes the Secretary to grant a permit for any taking otherwise prohibited by 9(a)(1)(B) "if such taking is incidental to, and not the purpose of, the carrying out of an otherwise lawful activity."

In addition to the prohibition on takings, the Act provides several other protections for endangered species. Section 4 commands the Secretary to identify species of fish or wildlife that are in danger of extinction and to publish from time to time lists of all species he determines to be endangered or threatened. Section 5 authorizes the Secretary, in cooperation with the States, to acquire land to aid in preserving such species. Section 7 requires federal agencies to ensure that none of their activities, including the granting of licenses and permits, will jeopardize the continued existence of endangered species "or result in the destruction or adverse modification of habitat of such species which is determined by the Secretary . . . to be critical."

The Case

Respondents in this action are small landowners, logging companies, and families dependent on the forest products industries in the Pacific Northwest and in the Southeast, and organizations that represent their interests. They brought this declaratory judgment action against petitioners, the Secretary of the Interior and the Director of the Fish and Wildlife Service, in the United States District Court for the District of Columbia to challenge the statutory validity of the Secretary's regulation defining "harm," particularly the inclusion of habitat modification and degradation in the definition. Respondents challenged the regulation on its face. Their complaint alleged that application of the "harm" regulation to the red-cockaded woodpecker, an endangered species, and the northern spotted owl, a threatened species, had injured them economically.

Respondents advanced three arguments to support their submission that Congress did not intend the word "take" in [Section] 9 to include habitat modification, as the Secretary's "harm" regulation provides. First, they correctly noted that language in the Senate's original version of the ESA would have defined "take" to include "destruction, modification, or curtailment of [the] habitat or range" of fish or wildlife, but the Senate deleted that language from the bill before enacting it. Second, respondents argued that Congress intended the Act's express authorization for the Federal Government to buy private land in order to prevent habitat degradation in [Section] 5 to be the exclusive check against habitat modification on private property. Third, because the Senate added the term "harm" to the definition of "take" in a floor amendment without debate, respondents argued that the court should not interpret the term so expansively as to include habitat modification.

The District Court considered and rejected each of respondents' arguments, finding "that Congress intended an expansive interpretation of the word 'take,' an interpretation that encompasses habitat modification." . . .

A divided panel of the Court of Appeals initially affirmed the judgment of the District Court. After granting a petition for rehearing, however, the panel reversed. . . .

A Reasonable Interpretation of "Harm"

We may appropriately make certain factual assumptions in order to frame the legal issue. First, we assume respondents have no desire to harm either the red-cockaded woodpecker or the spotted owl; they merely wish to continue logging activities that would be entirely proper if not prohibited by the ESA. On the other hand, we must assume [for the sake of argument] that those activities will have the effect, even though

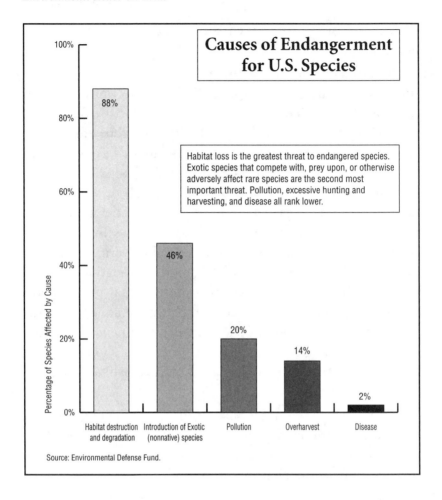

Causes of Endangerment for U.S. Species

Habitat loss is the greatest threat to endangered species. Exotic species that compete with, prey upon, or otherwise adversely affect rare species are the second most important threat. Pollution, excessive hunting and harvesting, and disease all rank lower.

Percentage of Species Affected by Cause

- Habitat destruction and degradation: 88%
- Introduction of Exotic (nonnative) species: 46%
- Pollution: 20%
- Overharvest: 14%
- Disease: 2%

Source: Environmental Defense Fund.

unintended, of detrimentally changing the natural habitat of both listed species and that, as a consequence, members of those species will be killed or injured. Under respondents' view of the law, the Secretary's only means of forestalling that grave result—even when the actor knows it is certain to occur—is to use his [Section] 5 authority to purchase the lands on which the survival of the species depends. The Secretary, on the other hand, submits that the [Section] 9 prohibition on takings, which Congress defined to include "harm," places on respondents a duty to avoid harm that habitat alteration will cause the birds unless respondents first obtain a permit pursuant to [Section] 10.

The text of the Act provides three reasons for concluding that the Secretary's interpretation is reasonable. First, an ordinary understanding of the word "harm" supports it. The dictionary definition of the verb form of "harm" is "to cause hurt or damage to: injure." In the context of the ESA, that definition naturally encompasses habitat modification that results in actual injury or death to members of an endangered or threatened species. . . .

Second, the broad purpose of the ESA supports the Secretary's decision to extend protection against activities that cause the precise harms Congress enacted the statute to avoid. In *TVA [Tennessee Valley Authority] v. Hill,* (1978), we described the Act as "the most comprehensive legislation for the preservation of endangered species ever enacted by any nation." Whereas predecessor statutes enacted in 1966 and 1969 had not contained any sweeping prohibition against the taking of endangered species except on federal lands, the 1973 Act applied to all land in the United States and to the Nation's territorial seas. As stated in [Section] 2 of the Act, among its central purposes is "to provide a means whereby the ecosystems upon which endangered species and threatened species depend may be conserved. . . ."

In *Hill,* we construed [Section] 7 as precluding the completion of the Tellico Dam because of its predicted impact on the survival of the snail darter. Both our holding and the language in our opinion stressed the importance of the statutory policy. "The plain intent of Congress in enacting this statute," we recognized, "was to halt and reverse the trend toward species extinction, whatever the cost. This is reflected not only in the stated policies of the Act, but in literally every section of the statute." Although the [Section] 9 "take" prohibition was not at issue in *Hill,* we took note of that prohibition, placing particular emphasis on the Secretary's inclusion of habitat modification in his definition of "harm." In light of that provision for habitat protection, we could "not understand how TVA intends to operate Tellico Dam without 'harming' the snail darter." Congress' intent to provide comprehensive protection for endangered and threatened species supports the permissibility of the Secretary's "harm" regulation.

Respondents advance strong arguments that activities that cause minimal or unforeseeable harm will not violate the Act as construed in the "harm" regulation. Respondents, however, . . . ask us to invalidate the Secretary's understanding of "harm" in every circumstance, even when an actor knows that an activity, such as draining a pond, would actually result in the extinction of a listed species by destroying its habitat. Given Congress' clear expression of the ESA's broad purpose to protect endangered and threatened wildlife, the Secretary's definition of "harm" is Reasonable. . . .

A Broad Definition of "Take"

Our conclusion that the Secretary's definition of "harm" rests on a permissible construction of the ESA gains further support from the legislative history of the statute. The Committee Reports accompanying the bills that became the ESA do not specifically discuss the meaning of "harm," but they make clear that Congress intended "take" to apply broadly to cover indirect as well as purposeful actions. The Senate Report stressed that "'[t]ake' is defined . . . in the broadest possible manner to include every conceivable way in which a person can 'take' or attempt to 'take' any fish or wildlife." The House Report stated that "the broadest possible terms" were used to define restrictions on takings. The House Report underscored the breadth of the "take" definition by noting that it included "harassment, whether intentional or not." The Report explained that the definition "would allow, for example, the Secretary to regulate or prohibit the activities of birdwatchers where the effect of those activities might disturb the birds and make it difficult for them to hatch or raise their young." These comments, ignored in the dissent's welcome but selective foray into legislative history, support the Secretary's interpretation that the term "take" in [Section] 9 reached far more than the deliberate actions of hunters and trappers. . . .

A Reasonable Interpretation

When it enacted the ESA, Congress delegated broad administrative and interpretive power to the Secretary. The task of defining and listing endangered and threatened species requires an expertise and attention to detail that exceeds the normal province of Congress. Fashioning appropriate standards for issuing permits under [Section] 10 for takings that would otherwise violate [Section] 9 necessarily requires the exercise of broad discretion. The proper interpretation of a term such as "harm" involves a complex policy choice. When Congress has entrusted the Secretary with broad discretion, we are especially reluctant to substitute our views of wise policy for his. In this case, that reluctance accords with our conclusion, based on the text, structure, and legislative history of the ESA, that the Secretary reasonably construed the intent of Congress when he defined "harm" to include "significant habitat modification or degradation that actually kills or injures wildlife."

In the elaboration and enforcement of the ESA, the Secretary and all persons who must comply with the law will confront difficult questions of proximity and degree; for, as all recognize, the Act encompasses a vast range of economic and social enterprises and endeavors. These questions must be addressed in the usual course of the law, through case-by-case resolution and adjudication.

The judgment of the Court of Appeals is reversed.

It is so ordered.

> "The Endangered Species Act ... places upon the public at large, rather than ... individual landowners, the cost of preserving the habitat of endangered species."

Dissenting Opinion: Landowners Are Not Responsible for Protecting Endangered Species

Antonin Scalia

The following viewpoint is excerpted from Justice Antonin Scalia's dissent to the U.S. Supreme Court's 1995 ruling in Babbitt v. Sweet Home Chapter of Communities for a Great Oregon. *In Scalia's opinion it is economically burdensome for individual landowners to refrain from modifying the habitats of endangered species. He argues that when it created the Endangered Species Act, Congress intended the public, not private landowners, to preserve such habitat through government purchase of the land. Moreover, Scalia maintains that when it prohibits "taking" or "harming" endangered species, the act refers to direct actions such as hunting and killing. He insists it is illogical to define* harm *as habitat modification. Scalia has served on the U.S. Supreme Court since 1975. He is widely considered to be one of the most conservative judges on the Court.*

I think it unmistakably clear that the legislation at issue here (1) forbade the hunting and killing of endangered animals, and (2) provided federal lands and federal funds for the ac-

Antonin Scalia, dissenting opinion, *Babbitt v. Sweet Home Chapter of Communities for a Great Oregon,* 515 U.S. 687, June 29, 1995.

quisition of private lands, to preserve the habitat of endangered animals. The Court's holding that the hunting and killing prohibition incidentally preserves habitat on private lands imposes unfairness to the point of financial ruin—not just upon the rich, but upon the simplest farmer who finds his land conscripted to national zoological use. I respectfully dissent.

The Endangered Species Act of 1973 provides that "it is unlawful for any person subject to the jurisdiction of the United States to take any [protected] species within the United States." The term "take" is defined as "to harass, harm, pursue, hunt, shoot, wound, kill, trap, capture, or collect, or to attempt to engage in any such conduct." The challenged regulation[1] defines "harm" thus:

> "'Harm' in the definition of 'take' in the Act means an act which actually kills or injures wildlife. Such act may include significant habitat modification or degradation where it actually kills or injures wildlife by significantly impairing essential behavioral patterns, including breeding, feeding or sheltering." . . .

Misinterpretation of the Endangered Species Act

The regulation has three features which, for reasons I shall discuss at length below, do not comport with the statute. First, it interprets the statute to prohibit habitat modification that is no more than the cause-in-fact of death or injury to wildlife. Any "significant habitat modification" that in fact produces that result by "impairing essential behavioral patterns" is made unlawful, regardless of whether that result is intended or even foreseeable, and no matter how long the chain of causality between modification and injury. . . .

---

1. The challenged regulation is the definition of "harm" created by the secretary of the interior, one of the people responsible for enforcing the Endangered Species Act.

Second, the regulation does not require an "act": the Secretary's officially stated position is that an omission will do. . . .

The third and most important unlawful feature of the regulation is that it encompasses injury inflicted, not only upon individual animals, but upon populations of the protected species. "Injury" in the regulation includes "significantly impairing essential behavioral patterns, including breeding," Impairment of breeding does not "injure" living creatures; it prevents them from propagating, thus "injuring" a population of animals which would otherwise have maintained or increased its numbers. . . .

None of these three features of the regulation can be found in the statutory provisions supposed to authorize it. The term "harm" has no legal force of its own. An indictment or civil complaint that charged the defendant with "harming" an animal protected under the Act would be dismissed as defective, for the only operative term in the statute is to "take." If "take" were not elsewhere defined in the Act, none could dispute what it means, for the term is as old as the law itself. To "take," when applied to wild animals, means to reduce those animals, by killing or capturing, to human control. . . . That meaning fits neatly with the rest of 1538(a)(1) [of the Endangered Species Act], which makes it unlawful not only to take protected species, but also to import or export them; to possess, sell, deliver, carry, transport, or ship any taken species, and to transport, sell, or offer to sell them in interstate or foreign commerce. The taking prohibition, in other words, is only part of the regulatory plan of 1538(a)(1), which covers all the stages of the process by which protected wildlife is reduced to man's dominion and made the object of profit. It is obvious that "take" in this sense—a term of art deeply embedded in the statutory and common law concerning wildlife—describes a class of acts (not omissions) done directly and intentionally (not indirectly and by accident) to particular animals (not populations of animals). . . .

The Meaning of "Harm"

The verb "harm" has a range of meaning: "to cause injury" at its broadest, "to do hurt or damage" in a narrower and more direct sense. See, e.g., *Webster, An American Dictionary of the English Language* (1828) ("Harm, v.t. To hurt; to injure; to damage; to impair soundness of body, either animal or vegetable"). *American College Dictionary* (1970) ("harm . . . n. injury; damage; hurt: to do him bodily harm") . . . . To define "harm" as an act or omission that, however remotely, "actually kills or injures" a population of wildlife through habitat modification, is to choose a meaning that makes nonsense of the word that "harm" defines—requiring us to accept that a farmer who tills his field and causes erosion that makes silt run into a nearby river which depletes oxygen and thereby "impairs [the] breeding" of protected fish, has "taken" or "attempted to take" the fish. It should take the strongest evidence to make us believe that Congress has defined a term in a manner repugnant to its ordinary and traditional sense.

Here the evidence shows the opposite. "Harm" is merely one of 10 prohibitory words in 1532(19) [of the act], and the other 9 fit the ordinary meaning of "take" perfectly. To "harass, pursue, hunt, shoot, wound, kill, trap, capture, or collect" are all affirmative acts (the provision itself describes them as "conduct,") which are directed immediately and intentionally against a particular animal—not acts or omissions that indirectly and accidentally cause injury to a population of animals. The Court points out that several of the words ("harass," "pursue," "wound," and "kill") "refer to actions or effects that do not require direct applications of force." That is true enough, but force is not the point. Even "taking" activities in the narrowest sense, activities traditionally engaged in by hunters and trappers, do not all consist of direct applications of force; pursuit and harassment are part of the business of "taking" the prey even before it has been touched. What the nine other words in 1532(19) have in common—and share with the narrower meaning of "harm" described above, but not with the [Secretary of the Interior's] ruthless dilation of the word—is the sense of affirmative conduct intentionally directed against a particular animal or animals. . . .

The Real Intent of the Senate

The Court maintains that the legislative history of the 1973 [Endangered Species] Act supports the Secretary's definition [of "take"]. Even if legislative history were a legitimate and reliable tool of interpretation (which I shall assume in order to rebut the Court's claim); and even if it could appropriately be resorted to when the enacted text is as clear as this; . . . here it shows quite the opposite of what the Court says. . . .

Both the Senate and House floor managers of the bill explained it in terms which leave no doubt that the problem of habitat destruction on private lands was to be solved principally by the land acquisition program of [the bill's Section]1534, while [Section] 1538 solved a different problem altogether—the problem of takings. Senator [John] Tunney stated:

> "Through [the] land acquisition provisions, we will be able to conserve habitats necessary to protect fish and wildlife from further destruction.

> "Although most endangered species are threatened primarily by the destruction of their natural habitats, a significant portion of these animals are subject to predation by man for commercial, sport, consumption, or other purposes. The provisions of [the bill] would prohibit the commerce in or the importation, exportation, or taking of endangered species . . . ."

The House floor manager, Representative Sullivan, put the same thought in this way:

"[T]he principal threat to animals stems from destruction of their habitat. ... [The bill] will meet this problem by providing funds for acquisition of critical habitat. ... It will also enable the Department of Agriculture to cooperate with willing landowners who desire to assist in the protection of endangered species, but who are understandably unwilling to do so at excessive cost to themselves. Another hazard to endangered species arises from those who would capture or kill them for pleasure or profit. There is no way that Congress can make it less pleasurable for a person to take an animal, but we can certainly make it less profitable for them to do so."

Habitat modification and takings, in other words, were viewed as different problems, addressed by different provisions of the Act. ...

A Public Responsibility

The Endangered Species Act is a carefully considered piece of legislation that forbids all persons to hunt or harm endangered animals, but places upon the public at large, rather than upon fortuitously accountable individual landowners, the cost of preserving the habitat of endangered species. There is neither textual support for, nor even evidence of congressional consideration of, the radically different disposition contained in the regulation that the Court sustains. For these reasons, I respectfully dissent.

> "[Sweet Home]*unfairly obligates prop-*
> *erty owners to preserve welcome mats*
> *for endangered or threatened species.*"

Sweet Home Unfairly Burdens Small Landowners

Bruce Fein

In the following viewpoint Bruce Fein argues that in the Sweet Home *decision, the Endangered Species Act is interpreted too broadly, placing an unfair burden of environmental preservation on private landowners. Fein agrees that habitat preservation may be an important part of preserving endangered species. However, he argues that this goal should be accomplished through land acquisition by the federal government, which is better able to bear the costs of this protection. It is unfair to place this burden on a handful of small landowners, he maintains, because it can prove economically devastating to these people. Fein is a lawyer and freelance writer specializing in legal issues.*

On June 29 [1995], the U.S. Supreme Court upheld a latitudinarian interpretation of the Endangered Species Act [ESA] of 1973 by the interior secretary that unfairly obligates private property owners to preserve welcome mats for endangered or threatened species. Writing for a 6-3 majority in *Babbitt v. Sweet Home Chapter of Communities for a Great Oregon* (June 29, 1995), Justice John Paul Stevens blessed the secretary's implementing regulation that prohibits owners from significantly modifying or degrading the habitat of a protected species if either the direct or indirect effect is to kill or injure wildlife.

Bruce Fein, "Landowners Lose Critical Court Case," *Human Events,* vol. 51, July 21, 1995, p. 14. Copyright © 1995 by Human Events, Inc. Reproduced by permission.

Enthusiasm Overrunning the Law

The *Sweet Home* ruling is a classic example of prevailing enthusiasm overrunning the law. Since enactment of the ESA more than two decades ago, social fretting over the environment has become epidemic, and customary standards of scientific objectivity and reliability have been compromised to further politically fetching agendas—for example, the ozone depletion scare. The law lacks any tough interpretive principles. It is thus predictable that environmental rulings will echo current orthodoxies.

The ESA prohibits the taking of any species of fish or wildlife listed by the secretary, and the term "take" is defined by the statute to mean "harass, harm, pursue, hunt shoot, wound, kill, trap, capture, or collect . . . ." The secretary amplified on the meaning of "harm" in a regulation to include "significant habitat modification or degradation where it actually kills or injures wildlife by significantly impairing essential behavioral patterns, including breeding, feeding or sheltering."

An Outlandish Conclusion

Small landowners, logging companies and families dependent on the forest products industry in the Pacific Northwest and the Southeast brought suit challenging the scope of the regulation; it had arrested the use of their land without government compensation for the crime of attractiveness to the endangered red-cockaded woodpecker and the threatened northern spotted owl. A federal appeals court sustained the challenge, but the Supreme Court reversed.

Justice Stevens denied that Congress intended to confine the meaning of "harm" to intentional killings or injuries to wildlife like its sister terms "to shoot, wound, capture," etc. Significant habitat modification undertaken for innocent reasons, he elaborated, may nonetheless constitute harm if its predictable effect is unfriendly to listed species, including the impairment of breeding. That conclusion, however, seems outlandish.

The 9th U.S. Circuit Court of Appeals had earlier upheld that octopus-like reach of "harm" in rebuking a state agency for permitting feral sheep to eat mamanenaio seedlings that when fully blossomed into forest trees, might have fed and sheltered the endangered pallia bird. And land that provides a recreational euphoria to listed species must remain undisturbed if the secretary concludes that such psychic buoyancy stimulates mating. The ordinary landowner or developer typically cannot afford the expense and years of delay entailed by a court challenge to the secretary's overreaching; they thus will accept a compromise of their legal rights and curtail some economic uses of their land to accommodate the secretary's demands.

Unfairly Burdening Citizens

If Congress intended the ESA to inflict such iniquity, Stevens should not be pummeled for being the messenger bearing the bad news. But congressional intent seemed to the contrary. The statute expressly authorizes the secretary to forestall habitat destruction on private lands through land acquisition: The floor manager of the bill in the Senate explained: "Through [the] land acquisition provisions, we will be able to conserve habitats necessary to protect fish and wildlife from further destruction." The House floor manager chorused: "[T]he principal threat to animals stems from destruction of their habitat. ... [The bill] will meet this problem by providing funds for acquisition of critical habitat." The ESA also expressly prohibits federal agency action from destroying or adversely modifying critical habitat without any corresponding prohibition on private enterprise. In other words, Congress deliberated carefully over preservation and chose land acquisition in lieu of economically crippling restrictions on land use when private property was implicated. That conclusion also fits harmoniously with the ethical and constitutional canon that one or a handful of citizens should not be saddled with the costs of providing a benefit, i.e., habitat preservation, to be enjoyed by the public generally.

"The Sweet Home *majority failed to recognize [biophilia] . . . and, in so doing, crafted a narrow interpretation of harm."*

Sweet Home's Protection of Endangered Species Is Too Narrow

L. Misha Preheim

While Babbitt v. Sweet Home Chapter of Communities for a Great Oregon *was decided in favor of protecting the habitats of endangered species, it relied on an overly narrow definition of habitat harm, maintains attorney L. Misha Preheim in the following viewpoint. He believes that in order to effectively protect endangered species, the Endangered Species Act must be interpreted in light of biophilia—the idea that humanity has an inherent connection with nature. This concept is widely recognized in many other disciplines and professions, he argues, and the courtroom should be no different. By failing to recognize biophilia, says Preheim, the Court is isolating itself from the realities of the scientific, economic, artistic, and religious world. He also argues that humanity will be harmed by the failure to protect the natural environment with which it shares a connection. Preheim is an attorney with Swidler Berlin, a Washington, D.C.–based law firm.*

It is estimated that we share the planet with between ten and one hundred million other species. Surprisingly, humans have given names to approximately 1.4 million species, a fraction of the total. We have, however, brought about the extinc-

L. Misha Preheim, "Biophilia, the Endangered Species Act, and a New Endangered Species Paradigm," *William and Mary Law Review,* vol. 42, March 2001, p. 1,053. Copyright © 2001 by *William and Mary Law Review,* College of William and Mary, Marshall Wythe School of Law. Reproduced by permission.

tion of an estimated 10% of the species that existed before humanity came on the scene, and it is predicted that another 20% will be lost in the next thirty years. One scholar has noted that "[t]he extinction event now taking place rivals the five great extinctions that have occurred in the earth's geologic history, only this time it is humans, not asteroids, that are the cause." Humanity has begun to recognize this catastrophe and, in some cases, has taken action. The Endangered Species Act (ESA) is one immediate, and potentially powerful, response to the extinction of species in the United States.

Unfortunately, the recent failure of the judiciary to interpret the ESA more expansively has limited the Act's ability to preserve species. This failure is reflected in the courts' inability to properly account for humanity's intrinsic connection with nature when determining what constitutes "harm" under the ESA. If the courts continue the perpetuation of a myopic understanding of the interplay between human life and the environment, it is humanity that inevitably will be affected.

Biophilia

The inherent connection that humanity maintains with nature, christened "biophilia" by the Harvard biologist Edward Wilson, provides the impetus for an argument that courts should rethink the way in which they have interpreted the ESA. Put simply, the intrinsic affiliation with nature that exists within the human species calls for an expansive interpretation of the ESA. This expansion would result in a definition of harm that recognizes that species must be protected from the potential, albeit conceivably uncertain, harm that habitat destruction can effect. This [viewpoint] argues that biophilia provides the foundation for a judicial expansion of the definition of "harm" under the ESA....

The ESA provides that no one shall "harm" a species that has been listed as endangered or threatened.... The Supreme Court's decision in *Babbitt v. Sweet Home Chapter of Commu-*

nities for a Great Oregon is perhaps the most important case in this area of law. . . . The *Sweet Home* court failed to recognize biophilia and, in so doing, permitted an overly narrow definition of "take" under the ESA. Had the Court recognized the intrinsic connection between humanity and nature, it would have concluded that "harm" to a species can occur in a myriad of ways far short of "'significant habitat modification or degradation that actually kills or injures wildlife.'". . .

What Is Biophilia?

In *Biophilia,* the biologist Edward O. Wilson presents the argument that human beings have an intrinsic connection with nature. Biophilia, he explains, is "the innate tendency to focus on life and lifelike processes.". . .

This simple, yet elegant concept—that human beings have an innate, genetic connection with nature—suggests astounding ramifications. Biophilia encompasses every action we take: every house we build, every painting we create, and every poem we write is shaped by our affiliation with the natural world and with other life forms. . . .

Thus, through our common DNA and through millions of years of co-evolution, we invariably have developed a connection with other species. The evidence of biophilia is not speculative but rather quite concrete. Cultural norms and patterns indicate that biophilia is ubiquitous to the human Species. . . .

Evidence of the Tenability of Biophilia

The legal world stands alone by failing to adopt biophilia or even make reference to it when reaching decisions that affect the survival of species. The theory of biophilia is not cited in any reported federal case. This might give the indication that biophilia and its architect, Edward Wilson, are not taken seriously in the scientific world or in other academic areas. Reality tells a different story: recognition of biophilia is prevalent in many academic disciplines, including economics, sociology, architecture, and mythology.

Within the economic field, there are a number of methodologies that have been developed to value the environment. Contingent valuation, for example, uses social survey techniques to ascertain how we value the natural world. . . . Contingent valuation studies indicate that human beings place a high value on the natural world. For example, one willingness-to-pay study estimated that the elephants in Kenya provide a value of $25 million per annum, "a sum almost ten times the value of poached ivory exports."

Furthermore, the economic value of ecotourism is high, especially on a global scale. [According to author Stephen R. Kellert] "[N]ature and wildlife tourism may now account for as much as 10 percent of the $300 billion world tourism market, growing at an estimated 10 to 20 percent rate in recent years." In a recent [1999] public opinion survey, 63% of respondents cited "'the beauty of nature'" as a reason for protecting the environment. It is also estimated that perhaps 5% to 10% of the American population are active birdwatchers. Americans speak with their wallets; the value that we place on the environment demonstrates our affiliation with nature.

In addition to economists, architects, particularly landscape architects, have long recognized the value of the natural world. [Filmmaker] Woody Allen is probably not an avid birdwatcher—he once said that "[n]ature and I are two"—yet Allen himself lives in a city (New York) that preserves some of the most valuable land in the world as parkland. . . .

Psychological studies also support the significance of biophilia. For example, studies have indicated that natural settings, particularly those with "savanna-like properties or non-turbulent water features," provide humans with restorative benefits. This psychological connection blends with landscape architecture. "During the last two centuries, in several countries, the idea that exposure to nature fosters psychological well-being, reduces the stresses of urban living, and promotes physical health has formed part of the justification for providing parks and other nature in cities and preserving wilderness for public use."

The religious world is also chock-full of biophilia. [According to Genesis 6:19 in the Bible, God said to Noah,] "And of every living thing of all flesh, two of every sort shalt thou bring into the ark, to keep them alive with thee; they shall be male and female." Noah was instructed to include not just "charismatic megafauna" on the ark. "Of fowls after their kind, and of cattle after their kind, of every creeping thing of the earth after his kind, two of every sort shall come unto thee, to keep them alive." . . .

Judiciary in Retreat: Confining the Concept of Harm

Perhaps most disturbing is the fact that the judiciary recently has begun to question the prohibition on balancing economic interests with environmental concerns under the ESA. In *Babbitt v. Sweet Home,* parties who were dependent on the forest products industry brought suit against the Department of the Interior, arguing that the Secretary's[1] definition of "take" was broader than Congress intended when it enacted the ESA. The ESA defines 'take' as to "harass, harm, pursue, hunt, shoot, wound, kill, trap, capture, or collect, or to attempt to engage in any such conduct." The Secretary of the Interior further defined harm to include "'significant habitat modification or degradation where it actually kills or injures wildlife by significantly impairing essential behavioral patterns, including breeding, feeding, or sheltering.'". . .

The Court cited three reasons why the Secretary's interpretation of the Act was reasonable. First, the Court explained that an ordinary understanding of the word "harm" supported this interpretation. Second, the Court explained that:

---

1. One of the people responsible for enforcing the ESA.

the broad purpose of the ESA supports the Secretary's decision to extend protection against activities that cause theprecise harms Congress enacted the statute to avoid. In *TVA [Tennessee Valley Authority] v. Hill*, we described the Act as "the most comprehensive legislation for the preservation of endangered species ever enacted by any nation.". . . As stated in [section] 2 of the Act, among its central purposes is "to provide a means whereby the ecosystems upon which endangered species and threatened species depend may be conserved . . . ."

The Court went on to explain that in *TVA*, it recognized that "[t]he plain intent of Congress in enacting this statute . . . was to halt and reverse the trend toward species extinction, whatever the cost. This is reflected not only in the stated policies of the Act, but in literally every section of the statute."

The third reason recognized by the Court was the fact that Congress authorized "the Secretary to issue permits for takings that [section] 9(a)(1)(B) would otherwise prohibit, 'if such taking [was] incidental to . . . the carrying out of an otherwise lawful activity . . . .'" This exception suggests that Congress itself felt that [section] 9(a)(1)(B) prohibited indirect takings.

Sweet Home embodies an overly narrow concept of harm that fails to consider biophilia. All three of the reasons mentioned by the Court give support to an even broader interpretation of the ESA. The purpose of the ESA, as embodied by biophilia, suggests a decision more in line with Congressional intent.

Justice O'Connor, in her concurrence, also failed to recognize the interconnectedness that biophilia suggests. She wrote that:

Proximate causation is not a concept susceptible of precise definition. It is easy enough, of course, to identify the extremes. The farmer whose fertilizer is lifted by a tornado from tilled fields and deposited miles away in a wildlife refuge cannot, by any stretch of the term, be considered the proximate cause of death or injury to protected species occasioned thereby. At the same time, the landowner who drains a pond on his property, killing endangered fish in the process, would likely satisfy any formulation of the principle. We have recently said that proximate causation "normally eliminates the bizarre. . . ." Proximate causation depends to a great extent on considerations of the fairness of imposing liability for remote consequences.

If Congress based the ESA on a biophilic purpose, this should play a part in considering when a species is harmed; biophilic harm to humans is a critical element of judicial consideration of the ESA. O'Connor and the *Sweet Home* majority failed to recognize Congress's biophilic intent and, in so doing, crafted a narrow interpretation of harm that ignores the importance of habitat preservation in ameliorating potential future harm to species. . . .

A New Endangered Species Paradigm

There are therefore three reasons why biophilia should be applied to the ESA. First, one of the primary purposes behind the ESA is a biophilic one; Congress considered humanity's connection with the natural world as intrinsic to the Act. Second, the recognition of biophilia, in one form or another, is commonplace in other academic disciplines and professions. From religion to architecture, biophilia permeates our lives and it is anomalous for the judiciary to stand alone in failing to recognize the doctrine. Finally, adopting biophilia in the courtroom may not be such a momentous leap after all; recognition of humanity's aesthetic valuation of nature supports the inclusion of biophilic considerations in the judicial decision-making process.

When considering cases under the ESA, courts should look to biophilia as a core purpose behind the Act. Decisions should be consistent with this purpose and should reflect the connection that humanity has with the natural world. Biophilia lends support to a revised definition of harm that recognizes habitat destruction and potential future harm as critical to the core purpose of the ESA.

Biophilia should be viewed as a tool to be used to better understand and evaluate the ESA. Humanity's innate connection with nature is something that needs to be recognized by the courts. Such an important concept should not be overlooked when determining whether the courts are fulfilling congressional intent.

> *"The Endangered Species Act . . . may ac-
> tually do a disservice to the species [it] is
> supposed to protect."*

The *Sweet Home* Decision
Discourages Conservation

Daniel R. Simmons and Randy T. Simmons

*In the following viewpoint Daniel R. Simmons and Randy T.
Simmons argue that while it is designed to protect endangered
species and their habitats, in many cases the Endangered Species
Act actually results in harm to endangered species on private
property. They explain that because of court decisions such as*
Babbitt v. Sweet Home Chapter of Communities for a Great
Oregon, *property owners with endangered species on their land
face severe restrictions on how they can use that land—restrictions that can cause economic ruin. Thus, these owners often
take actions to discourage endangered species from residing there
in the first place, say the authors. The authors thus conclude that
harsh restrictions, such as* Sweet Home's *prohibition on habitat
modification, may not be the most effective way to save endangered species. Daniel R. Simmons is a research fellow at the Mer-
catus Center in Virginia. Randy T. Simmons is a professor of political science at Utah State University and a senior fellow at the
Political Economy Research Center.*

On December 28 [2003], the Endangered Species Act (ESA)
turns 30. One of the biggest controversies over the ESA
has been its effect on private property. Many analysts suggest
that the act's restrictions on property rights actually discourage conservation, which has prompted the U.S. Fish and Wild-

Daniel R. Simmons and Randy T. Simmons, "The Endangered Species Act Turns 30,"
Regulation, vol. 26, Winter 2003, p. 6. Copyright © 2003 by the Cato Institute. All
rights reserved. Reproduced by permission.

life Service (FWS) to promulgate new rules to address that issue. The proposed new rules attempt to give private property owners some assurance that after the FWS regulates their private property, it will not come back with more restrictive regulations.

Private Property

There are two key sections in the ESA that give the FWS the regulatory authority to regulate private property: Sections 7 and 9. Section 9 prohibits the "taking" of an endangered or threatened species, where "taking" means "to harass, harm, pursue, hunt, shoot, wound, kill, trap, capture, or collect, or to attempt to engage in such conduct." The FWS expansively defines "harm" to include modifying an endangered or threatened species' habitat.

Regulations based on this definition of harm are controversial because they are a form of national land-use control. This controversy reached the U.S. Supreme Court in the 1995 case *Babbitt v. Sweet Home.* In that case, the Court deferred to the FWS's interpretation of "harm," holding that the definition includes habitat modification.

In dissent, Justice Antonin Scalia argued that "the Court's holding that the hunting and killing prohibition incidentally preserves habitat on private lands imposes unfairness to the point of financial ruin—not just upon the rich, but upon the simplest farmer who finds his land conscripted to national zoological use." The *Sweet Home* decision, Environmental Defense attorney Michael Bean has explained, effectively means that "a forest landowner harvesting timber, a farmer plowing new ground, or developer clearing land for a shopping center stood in the same position as a poacher taking aim at a whooping crane." . . .

Effects on Landowners

Nearly 80 percent of all listed species occur partially or entirely on private lands. Many analysts agree with Bean that one overall effect of enforcing the ESA has been to create "unintended negative consequences, including antagonizing many of the landowners whose actions will ultimately determine the fate of many species." Bean underscored those problems in a 1994 speech at a training and education seminar sponsored by the FWS for government employees. There is, he said, "increasing evidence that at least some private landowners are actively managing their land so as to avoid potential endangered species problems." By that, he meant the landowners are removing habitat that might attract an endangered species. He emphasized, however, that those actions are "not the result of malice toward the environment" but are instead "fairly rational decisions motivated by a desire to avoid potentially significant economic constraints." He even said they are a "predictable response to the familiar perverse incentives that sometimes accompany regulatory programs, not just the endangered species program but others."

The National Association of Home Builders explains in its *Developer's Guide to Endangered Species Regulation,*

> Unfortunately, the highest level of assurance that a property owner will not face an ESA issue is to maintain the property in a condition such that protected species cannot occupy the property. Agricultural farming, denuding of property, and managing the vegetation in ways that prevent the presence of such species are often employed in areas where ESA conflicts are known to occur.

Making land inhospitable to endangered species is one manifestation of what is now known as "preemptive habitat destruction."

Although there are many stories of such practices, there are few studies that rely on hard data. There is, however, one systematic study of preemptive habitat destruction that examines timber-harvest practices in forests occupied by red-cockaded woodpeckers. In their 2000 paper "Preemptive Habitat Destruction under the Endangered Species Act," Dean Lueck of Montana State University and Jeffrey A. Michael of Towson University (Md.) used data from over 1,000 individual forest plots from the U.S. Forest Service's Forest Inventory and Analysis and a 1997–98 North Carolina State University survey of over 400 landowners. Red-cockaded woodpeckers provide a good test of claims that the ESA produces perverse incentives. The birds have been listed as an endangered species for 30 years. They live in colonies consisting of the breeding pair, the current year's offspring, and the sons of the breeding male. They depend on mature stands of southern pine—they only nest or roost in cavities in living pine trees that are at least 60 years old.

That provides a clearly measurable test of habitat modification. Lueck and Michael found that trees close to colonies of red-cockaded woodpeckers are logged prematurely. That is, the trees are not allowed to get old enough to provide nesting cavities for the birds. As distance from a known colony of woodpeckers increases, the chance of harvest decreases and the age at which the forest is harvested increases. The authors conclude, "This evidence from two separate micro-level data sets indicates habitat has been reduced on private land because of the ESA." In fact, enough habitat was reduced because of the ESA between 1984 and 1990 to have supported a woodpecker population sufficient to meet the FWS's recovery goals for the species, according to one set of Lueck and Michael's estimates.

It appears that the answer to how people react to standing "in the same position as a poacher taking aim at a whooping crane" is that at least some of them take legal and even illegal preemptive actions. Potential results include active habitat destruction, passive non-protection, and an unwillingness to undertake improvements. Others take direct actions against the species and "shoot, shovel, and shut up," as the saying goes. It would be surprising if other regulations did not produce simi-

Red-cockaded woodpeckers nest in pine trees that are at least sixty years old. Premature logging in their habitat threatens the species' survival. U.S. Fish and Wildlife Service/John and Karen Hollingsworth

lar results; Lueck and Michael note, for instance, that when stricter wetland draining rules were proposed in North Carolina, "landowners went on a drainage and ditching spree." In just a few months, 15–20 times more wetlands were developed than were normally developed in an entire year. . . .

Saving Species?

The number of endangered species listed in the United States has increased from 114 in 1973 to 1,263 today [2003]. The Fish and Wildlife Service's most recent report on the status of endangered species found that only nine percent of those listed under the ESA are improving and only 30 percent of listed species are stable. Since 1973, only 33 species have been delisted, seven because they went extinct and 12 more because they should not have been listed in the first place. Of the remaining 14 delisted species, three are kangaroo species that were delisted when the Australian government changed its management practices. Six more may be cases of data error, which is certainly the case with the gray whale and American alligator. The brown pelican's and Arctic peregrine falcon's recoveries have far more to do with the ban on the insecticide DDT than with the Endangered Species Act. There are very few justifiable claims that the ESA retrieves species from the brink of extinction and returns them to viability.

Measuring success by numbers of species delisted or by visible reintroduction programs may be the wrong measurements. After all, only seven of the species listed since the act was signed in 1973 are now extinct, and most species that have recovered were listed only after they were well on the way to extinction. But it is striking that none of the recovered species reemerged because of the regulation of private property. Private property regulations are not a primary, or even a significant, cause for those recoveries.

A Disservice to Endangered Species

Over the last 30 years, the Endangered Species Act has proved to be a powerful tool for controlling land use. Unfortunately, this not only impinges on private landowners' rights, but may actually do a disservice to the species the ESA is supposed to protect. None of the species removed from the endangered species list were removed because the FWS regulates private property. Any attempts to improve the ESA should recognize that fact.

Organizations to Contact

Cato Institute
1000 Massachusetts Ave. NW
Washington, DC 20001-5403
(202) 842-0200 • fax: (202) 842-3490
e-mail: cato@cato.org
Web site: www.cato.org

The Cato Institute is a libertarian public policy research foundation that aims to limit the role of government and protect civil liberties. The institute believes Environmental Protection Agency regulations are too stringent. Publications offered on its Web site include the bimonthly *Cato Policy Report,* the quarterly journal *Regulation,* and numerous books and articles.

Competitive Enterprise Institute (CEI)
1001 Connecticut Ave. NW, Suite 1250
Washington, DC 20036
(202) 331-1010 • fax: (202) 331-0640
e-mail: info@cei.org
Web site: www.cei.org

CEI is a nonprofit public policy organization dedicated to the principles of free enterprise and limited government. The institute believes private incentives and property rights, rather than government regulations, are the best way to protect the environment. CEI's publications include the newsletter *Monthly Planet, On Point* policy briefs, and the book *True State of the Planet.*

Environmental Protection Agency (EPA)
Ariel Ross Bldg., 1200 Pennsylvania Ave. NW
Washington, DC 20460
(202) 272-0167
Web site: www.epa.gov

The EPA is the federal agency in charge of protecting the environment and controlling pollution. The agency works toward these goals by enacting and enforcing regulations, identifying and fining polluters, assisting local businesses and local environmental agencies, and cleaning up polluted sites. The EPA publishes periodic reports and the monthly *EPA Activities Update.*

Environment Canada
351 St. Joseph Blvd., Gratineau, QC
 K1A OH3 Canada
(819) 997-2800 • fax: (819) 953-2225
e-mail: enviroinfo@ec.gc.ca
Web site: www.ec.gc.ca

Environment Canada is a department of the Canadian government. Its goal is the achievement of sustainable development in Canada through conservation and environmental protection. The department publishes reports, including "Environmental Signals 2003," and fact sheets on a number of topics such as pollution prevention.

Hudson Institute
Herman Kahn Center, Indianapolis, IN 46226
(317) 545-1000 • fax: (317) 545-1384
e-mail: johnmc@hii.hudson.org
Web site: www.hudson.org

The Hudson Institute is a public policy research center whose members are elected from academia, government, and industry. The institute promotes the power of the free market and human ingenuity to solve environmental problems. Its publications include the monthly *Outlook* and the monthly policy bulletin *Foresight.*

Natural Resources Defense Council (NRDC)
40 W. Twentieth St., New York, NY 10011
(212) 727-2700

e-mail: nrdcinfo@nrdc.org
Web site: www.nrdc.org

The NRDC is a nonprofit organization with more than four hundred thousand members. It uses laws and science to protect the environment, including wildlife and wild places. NRDC publishes the quarterly magazine *OnEarth* and hundreds of reports, including "Development and Dollars" and the annual "Testing the Waters."

Political Economy Research Center (PERC)
502 S. Nineteenth Ave., Bozeman, MT 59718
(406) 587-9591
e-mail: perc@perc.org
Web site: www.perc.org

PERC is a research and educational foundation that focuses primarily on environmental and natural resource issues. Its approach emphasizes the use of the free market and the importance of private property rights in protecting the environment. Publications include *PERC Viewpoint* and *PERC Reports*.

Sierra Club
85 Second St., 2nd Fl., San Francisco
 CA 94105
(415) 977-5500 • fax: (415) 977-5799
e-mail: information@sierraclub.org
Web site: www.sierraclub.org

The Sierra Club is a grassroots organization with chapters in every state that promotes the protection and conservation of natural resources. The organization maintains separate committees on air quality, global environment, and solid waste, among other environmental concerns, to help achieve its goals. It publishes books, fact sheets, the bimonthly magazine *Sierra* and the *Planet* newsletter, which appears several times a year.

Worldwatch Institute
1776 Massachusetts Ave. NW
 Washington, DC 20036-1904

(202) 452-1999 • fax: (202) 296-7365
e-mail: worldwatch@worldwatch.org
Web site: www.worldwatch.org

WorldWatch is a nonprofit public policy research organization dedicated to informing the public and policy makers about emerging problems and trends and the complex links between the environment and the economy. Its publications include *Vital Signs,* issued annually, the bimonthly magazine *World Watch,* the Environmental Alert series, and numerous policy papers, including "Unnatural Disasters" and "City Limits: Putting the Brakes on Sprawl."

For Further Research

Books

Uday Desai, ed., *Environmental Politics and Policy in Industrialized Countries.* Cambridge, MA: MIT Press, 2002.

William Dietrich, *The Final Forest: The Battle for the Last Great Trees of the Pacific Northwest.* New York: Penguin, 1993.

Michael P. Dombeck, Christopher A. Wood, and Jack E. Williams, *From Conquest to Conservation: Our Public Lands Legacy.* Washington, DC: Island, 2003.

Winston Harrington, Richard D. Morgenstern, and Thomas Sterner, *Choosing Environmental Policy: Comparing Instruments and Outcomes in the United States and Europe.* Washington, DC: Resources for the Future, 2004.

Thomas More Hoban and Richard Oliver Brooks, *Green Justice: The Environment and the Courts.* Boulder, CO: Westview, 1996.

David Hunter, James Salzman, and Durwood Zaelke, *International Environmental Law and Policy.* New York: Foundation Press, 2001.

Michael E. Kraft, *Environmental Policy and Politics.* Chicago: Longman, 2003.

Michael E. Kraft and Norman J. Vig, eds., *Environmental Policy in the 1990s: Reform or Reaction?* Washington, DC: CQ Press, 1997.

Judith A. Layzer, *The Environmental Case: Translating Values into Policy.* Washington, DC: CQ Press, 2002.

Richard J. Lazarus, *The Making of Environmental Law.* Chicago: University of Chicago Press, 2004.

Roy J. Lewicki, Barbara Gray, and Michael Elliot, eds., *Making Sense of Intractable Environmental Conflicts: Frames and Cases.* Washington, DC: Island Press, 2003.

Olga L. Moya and Andrew L. Fono, *Federal Environmental Law: The User's Guide*. St. Paul, MN: West Publishing, 1997.

Shannon C. Peterson, *Acting for Endangered Species: The Statutory Ark*. Lawrence: University Press of Kansas, 2002.

Paul Portney and Robert N. Stavins, *Public Policies for Environmental Protection*. Washington, DC: Resources for the Future, 2000.

Victor B. Scheffer, *The Shaping of Environmentalism in America*. Seattle: University of Washington Press, 1991.

Thomas F.P. Sullivan, *Environmental Law Handbook*. Rockville, MD: Government Institutes, 2001.

Larry Underwood, *Case Studies in Environmental Science*. Fort Worth, TX: Harcourt College, 2001.

Christina M. Valente and William D. Valente, *Introduction to Environmental Law and Policy: Protecting the Environment Through Law*. St. Paul, MN: West Publishing, 1995.

Norman J. Vig and Michael E. Kraft, eds., *Environmental Policy: New Directions for the Twenty-First Century*. Washington, DC: CQ Press, 2002.

Steven Lewis Yaffee, *The Wisdom of the Spotted Owl: Policy Lessons for a New Century*. Washington, DC: Island, 1994.

Periodicals

General Articles on the Environment

Doug Bandow, "Endangered Species Endanger Landowners' Rights," *Conservative Chronicle*, February 25, 2004.

Federico Cheever and Michael Balster, "The Take Prohibition in Section 9 of the Endangered Species Act: Contradictions, Ugly Ducklings, and Conservation of Species," *Environmental Law*, Spring 2004.

James W. Ely Jr., "Property Rights and Environmental Regulation: The Case for Preemption," *Harvard Journal of Law and Public Policy,* Fall 2004.

Deborah Gangloff, "Ecosystem Value and Trees: Greener, Cleaner, More Financially Savvy Environments Include Trees. The Evidence Is All Around Us," *American Forests,* Spring 2004.

Janet Larson, "The Sixth Great Extinction," *USA Today Magazine,* November 2004.

Thomas Lovejoy and J. Daniel Philips, "Seeing the Forest—Conservation on a Continental Scale," *Foreign Affairs,* July/August 2004.

Bradford C. Mank, "Standing and Global Warming: Is Injury to All Injury to None?" *Environmental Law,* Winter 2005.

Ian McEwan, "The Hot Breath of Civilization," *Los Angeles Times,* April 22, 2005.

New York Times, "An Endangered Act," July 5, 2005.

James M. Noble, "*Friends of the Earth v. Laidlaw* and the Increasingly Broad Standard for Citizen Standing to Sue in Environmental Litigation," *Natural Resources Journal,* Spring 2002.

Brian Nowicki, "Delays in Endangered Species Act Protections Lead to Extinctions," *Earth Island Journal,* Autumn 2004.

Fred Pearce, "Forest Dwellers Are Its Best Protectors," *New Scientist,* July 31, 2004.

Robert V. Percival, "'Greening' the Constitution: Harmonizing Environmental and Constitutional Values," *Environmental Law,* Fall 2002.

Zygmunt J.B. Plater, "Endangered Species Act Lessons over 30 Years, and the Legacy of the Snail Darter, a Small Fish in a Pork Barrel," *Environmental Law,* Spring 2004.

Rosalind Reeve, "At Risk," *World Today,* August/September 2004.

Elizabeth Royte, "Don't Spoil the Soil," *OnEarth*, Fall 2003.

J.B. Ruhl, "Endangered Species Act Innovations in the Post-Babbittonian Era—Are There Any?" *Duke Environmental Law & Policy Forum*, Spring 2004.

Rodger Schlickeisen, "The Endangered Species Act Turns 30," *Earth Island Journal*, Autumn 2004.

Scenic Hudson Preservation Conference v. Federal Power Commission (1965)

Environmental Law Reporter, "Calm After the Storm: Grandmother of All Lawsuits Settled By Mediation," March/April 1981.

Gladwin Hill, "Conservationists See Gains in U.S. Courts," *New York Times*, October 19, 1970.

Gladwin Hill, "Pollution Fight Set by Lawyers," *New York Times*, March 23, 1974.

David Sive, "Environmental Standing," *Natural Resources & Environment*, Fall 1995.

David Sive and Daniel Riesel, "A Grass-Roots Fire Spread Through the Law: Scenic Hudson Led, in Time, to Superfund," *National Law Journal*, November 29, 1993.

Seattle Audubon Society v. John L. Evans and Washington Contract Loggers Association (1991)

Timothy Egan, "Oregon, Foiling Forecasters, Thrives as It Protects Owls," *New York Times*, October 11, 1994.

Daniel Glick, "Having Owls and Jobs Too," *National Wildlife*, August/September 1995.

Ed Hunt, "Questioning the New Mythology," *Hunt and Peck*, September 22, 2000.

Claire Montgomery and Gardner M. Brown Jr., "Economics of Species Preservation," *Contemporary Economic Policy*, Vol. 10, 1992.

Brendon Swedlow, "Scientists, Judges, and Spotted Owls: Policymakers in the Pacific Northwest," *Duke Environmental Law & Policy Forum,* Spring 2003.

Lucas v. South Carolina Coastal Council (1992)

Caryn L. Beck-Dudley and James E. Macdonald, "*Lucas v. South Carolina Council,* Takings, and the Search for the Common Good," *American Business Law Journal,* Winter 1995.

Michael C. Blumm, "Property Myths, Judicial Activism, and the *Lucas* Case," *Environmental Law,* July 1993.

Christian Science Monitor, "A Troubling New Ruling on Property Rights," July 16, 1992.

William Funk, "Revolution or Restatement? Awaiting Answers to *Lucas'* Unanswered Questions," *Environmental Law,* July 1993.

Charlie B. Tyer, "Public Needs vs. Private Loss: Land Use Regulation and Property Rights," *International Journal of Public Administration,* 2000.

Wall Street Journal, "Property Gains," July 1, 1992.

Babbitt v. Sweet Home Chapter of Communities for a Great Oregon (1995)

Donald C. Dilworth, "High Court Decision Protecting Species May Endanger Law," *Trial,* September 1995.

Frona M. Powell, "Defining Harm Under the Endangered Species Act: Implications of *Babbitt v. Sweet Home,*" *American Business Law Journal,* Fall 1995.

David Salveson, "Endangered Species Get Supreme Court Reprieve," *Planning,* August 1995.

Roger Strelow, "Landowners Need Protection Too," *National Law Journal,* August 28, 1995.

Index

Marianne Jewell Memorial Library
Baker College of Muskegon
Michigan 49442